About the Author

Yanky Fachler received a Master's in Social Science in the UK and then worked in a variety of management roles in Israel before becoming a freelance copywriter. Now based in Dundalk, Ireland, Yanky (that **IS** his real name!) currently works as a motivational speaker, entrepreneurial trainer, life coach and marketing consultant in Ireland and abroad.

Also by Yanky Fachler

My Family Doesn't Understand Me!
The Vow

FIRE IN THE BELLY

An Exploration of the Entrepreneurial Spirit

Yanky Fachler

www.oaktreepress.com

OAK TREE PRESS

19 Rutland Street, Cork, Ireland
http://www.oaktreepress.com

Printed in the Republic of Ireland by ColourBooks.

Contents

Acknowledgements

Many lovely people inspired me to write this book. It all began with a 90-second phone call from my friend Alan Clark, who runs his own PR business in Scotland.

"You're an entrepreneur", he said. "You're an actor. You love an audience. You're in the image promotion field. Ergo, you are uniquely qualified to motivate other entrepreneurs. Think about it."

I did, and the result was a series of motivational entrepreneurship workshops that spawned this book.

Without my partner Mona's support and encouragement (she claims this book cost her a Scrabble partner), I could never have attempted this project.

The first colleague to suggest that the workshop material was eminently suitable for a book was Gráinne Harte, who has been a pillar of support since I arrived in Ireland. My Californian-based son Ashi (who describes himself as a fifth-generation entrepreneur) gave me valuable feedback, as did my daughter-in-law Jamie and my brother Meir.

John Teeling, the teetotal founder of the Cooley Distillery, kindly shared his comments on the manuscript and offered to write the Foreword. My esteemed papa, Eli Fachler, whose entrepreneurial example I belatedly came to emulate, also read the manuscript and made valuable comments.

I've always been intrigued by the stock phrase in every Acknowledgement: "The author bears sole responsibility for the finished product." Why does no one ever place the blame and responsibility squarely on the people who helped them? But now that I'm the one writing the book, I have no such inclination. I have enjoyed every minute I spent on the book, and I happily take responsibility for the contents.

DEDICATION

For Mona, Alan, E+E and A+A

Foreword

If you have got even this far in this book, then you are already halfway there. In our working lives, many of us have a nagging feeling of dissatisfaction; we may not be unhappy at work but we are not fulfilled. Some of us simply do not like working in organisations where we have no control over what we are doing. There is an answer: work for yourself. That's what this book is all about. It identifies the symptoms of unease, lays bare the concerns of people in the workplace and then puts forward an alternative.

This is a lifestyle book, not a "how to" manual or an academic thesis. The author refuses to accept tight definitions of entrepreneur, enterprise and risk-taking. He is right. For most of us, the hard part of becoming an entrepreneur is to get comfortable with the idea of being outside of the corporate world. Help is at hand. In chapter after chapter, your nagging worries are addressed in simple clear language. Read these chapters carefully and reflect. If the content strikes a chord, then you owe it to yourself and your family to give serious consideration to what you really want to do with your life.

Have you the "fire in your belly"? This is not the indigestion you will get from stress when any of a million things go wrong, but it is the Vision, the Concept — the idea in which you really believe and on which you are going to base your future.

Have you the guts to take the rough with the smooth? Be sure, there will be hard times and it will be up to you to battle through. Can you handle failure? It happens, accept it and move on.

Read the chapter "10 Don'ts". There is good advice there but maybe I'll add an "11th Don't" — Don't believe everything the experts say. I'm quoted in the chapter advising entrepreneurs to take time off and have a life. Yea, great idea! I took two days off in the year 2000. Am I dumb or something? Maybe, but after 30 years of enterprise I am blessed that I am still getting a huge buzz from coming to work every day. The projects I am in, and those new ones I am looking at, give me huge satisfaction. Why would I want to play golf when I can crawl down gold mines in Zimbabwe, watch piranhas in the stream beside our oil rig in Bolivia or sell whiskey from a stand in San Francisco?

If you are an entrepreneur, work is fun. You are needed. Despite the advances in recent years, Europeans still set up half as many new ventures as their US cousins. Entrepreneurs create wealth and jobs, large companies lose jobs and create little wealth.

Enjoy the book.

John Teeling
Chairman, Cooley Distillery

Chapter 1

Off the Ladder and Up the Wall

Leaving your salaried job to start your own business is in vogue. Lots of people are doing it, and according to research, 75% of salaried employees consider starting their own business at some time or another.

But what exactly does this involve? What sort of person should become an entrepreneur — and what sort of person shouldn't?

The ladder in the title of this chapter refers to the career ladder, the world of salaried employment. Up the wall refers to the commonly-held notion that anyone who wants to start their own business must be crazy.

This book looks at what happens when you swap the security of the ladder world for the risk and uncertainty of being your own boss.

We will explore the differences between a world where someone else decides how you spend your working hours, to one where you decide your own priorities.

We will also analyse why some people can have such violent allergic reactions to ladders, while others are happy to stay on a ladder all their lives.

I admit to being happily unemployable. I have spent 20 years of sleepless nights worrying about my own business. I have also spent 20 years of fulfilling days thanking my lucky stars that I don't work for anyone else.

REACHING PARTS OF THE ENTREPRENEUR'S SOUL THAT OTHER BOOKS FORGET

Go into any decent bookshop, and browse through the business section. You will find literally hundreds of different titles on the shelves. "How to" this, "how to" that. Everything from "How to make effective presentations" to "How to hire the right people".

You'll also find dozens of self-help books telling you "How to be your own boss". Nearly all of these titles follow a similar pattern.

They open with something on the entrepreneurial spirit — the actual decision to start your own business. Then they swiftly launch into a detailed explanation of all the critical management skills, business skills, people skills, time management skills, tax issues, access to funding and things like that. In other words, everything that you need to master if you want to be your own boss.

Some books devote just a sentence to this decision to become an entrepreneur, others a few paragraphs or a whole chapter.

To help you decide whether or not you are entrepreneurial material, some books even include one of those self-assessment tests that you can find in lifestyle magazines:

> "If you scored over 80, what are you waiting for! You're a natural entrepreneur — get out there and start your business today!"

> "If you scored below 40, maybe you should reconsider your decision to start your own business."

Anyone who has ever attended a Start Your Own Business programme will know that their focus is almost exclusively on skills. The emphasis is on the how and the what, not on the why. The emphasis is on what you have to **do**, not what you have to **be**, to start your own business.

The thinking behind this approach is that the decision to be your own boss is straightforward, and that the difficult part is to effectively and successfully run your own business. The underlying message seems to be: "You've decided to be an entrepreneur? Great — now let's talk about the skills you need to learn."

I think it's the other way round. I believe that the hard part is the realisation that you want to be an entrepreneur.

Once you make the decision to get off the employment ladder, I believe that anyone of average intelligence can learn the necessary business skills.

"How to" books and websites, and Start Your Own Business programmes, can prove most valuable in helping you to master these skills. But let's not confuse the cart with the horse. What is the point of teaching people entrepreneurial skills unless they first understand what starting a business involves on a personal level? On a feelings level? On an emotional level?

Pumping people with entrepreneurial skills, knowledge, facts and tips serves little purpose if you forget to check whether they ought to be entrepreneurs in the first place.

This book is dedicated to this neglected part of the entrepreneurial equation.

We will ask what it means to go out and do your own thing. We will attempt to get under the skin of those individuals — or maybe we should say individualists — who are thinking of leaving their salaried positions in order to start their own business.

We will analyse the "fire in the belly" that fuels the entrepreneurial urge. We will explore the thrill, the challenge, the fun — and yes, the problems too — of becoming an entrepreneur.

"Think you can or think you can't,
either way you'll be right."

— Henry Ford

I deliberately use the word explore. Not judge. In this book, entrepreneurs aren't the goodies and non-entrepreneurs aren't the baddies.

The relationship between the ladder and the entrepreneurial worlds is a dynamic one.

Most entrepreneurs start their working life on a ladder. Some people in the ladder world should never be tempted to work for themselves, and some entrepreneurs might be better off on a ladder. And many people in each world will spend a lifetime wondering if they belong in the other world.

Our particular focus will be people in the ladder world who want to start their own business. It is their perspective, their experiences and their expectations that will guide this exploration of the entrepreneurial spirit.

NO ONE CAN EVER GUARANTEE THAT YOUR BUSINESS VENTURE WILL PROSPER

It may be obvious, but I will say it anyway: however strong your desire to be your own boss, and however many entrepreneurial skills you possess, no one can ever guarantee that your business venture will prosper. However many "How to" books you read, and however many Start Your Own Business programmes you attend, an entrepreneurial mindset alone is not enough.

At the end of the day, your new enterprise has to be viable. Putting your money where your mouth is and opening your own business is great — but you still might not make it in the business world.

However, my intention in this book is not to dwell on the negative. Focusing exclusively on the risks is to miss the very essence of the entrepreneurial experience.

Because the decision to be your own boss is a leap of faith. It's about independence — emotional as well as financial. It's about embarking on an adventure.

Join me as we look at what makes entrepreneurs tick.

Chapter 2

Entrepreneurs —
A Question of Definition

*"Going into business for yourself,
becoming an entrepreneur, is the
modern-day equivalent of pioneering
on the old frontier."*

— Paula Nelson

Entrepreneurs are in fashion. We are flavour of the month. In the words of one business magazine, "*We admire their creativity, élan, and daring*".

But exactly what and who is an entrepreneur?

Much confusion still surrounds the term. Almost every entrepreneurial expert has a different definition of entrepreneurship.

Here's how the Kauffman Centre for Entrepreneurial Leadership in the USA defines an entrepreneur:

"Someone who is willing and eager to create a new venture in order to present a concept to the marketplace, someone who creates and manages change by pursuing opportunity, acting with passion for a purpose, living proactively, and leveraging resources to create value."

That's a bit of a mouthful, isn't it? Here are two more definitions:

"Someone who converts ideas into viable business by means of ingenuity, hard work, resilience, imagination and luck."

"Someone who, starting with nothing more than an idea for a new venture, has the ability to take it to the point at which the business can sustain itself financially."

Some entrepreneurship experts distinguish between what they term the old definition: *"Simply the process for starting a new business"* and the new definition: *"An opportunistic mindset and spirit."*

They also distinguish between entrepreneurial ventures and small businesses. True entrepreneurs, they claim, are driven by opportunity. They focus on innovation, they are determined to create new value by shaking up the marketplace, and they are determined to grow. Small businesses, or lifestyle businesses as they are termed, "simply" want to provide a job for themselves, to provide income for their family. Small businesses, these experts claim, tend to remain small.

I think that this nit-picking approach short-changes people who want to start their own business but who don't necessarily want to indulge in empire-building.

This may be about the different ways in which Americans and Europeans define an entrepreneur, but I suspect that lurking behind this approach is an assumption that it is exclusively financial success that determines whether or not a person is an entrepreneur. According to this way of thinking, if you are not a runaway success story, you forfeit the right to call yourself an entrepreneur.

To confuse the issue further, many experts now claim that you can be an entrepreneur in all walks of life: when you work in a large company, when you have your own business, or when you are at home raising kids.

Personally, I prefer more offbeat descriptions of the entrepreneur:

> *"The skydivers of the business world. The thrill of the jump is almost as important as the safe landing."*

> *"The last refuge of the trouble-making individual."*

But, for the purposes of this book, what we need is a simple, straightforward definition of entrepreneur. We need a definition that is broader than "being a financial success", but not so broad that it dilutes the true essence of entrepreneurship.

The working definition of entrepreneur that we will use is:

> *"Anyone who feels the urge to be their own boss and who starts their own business."*

This definition includes high tech, low tech and no tech. It includes people who want to work in services, as well as those who want to work in manufacturing. It includes people who want to work on their own (a one-person business, or soloist) and those who intend to employ staff. Our definition covers small businesses as well as companies that grow into big businesses. It includes bricks-and-mortar operations, click-and-order operations, and bricks 'n clicks operations.

> *"Whenever you see a successful business, someone made a courageous decision."*
>
> — Peter Drucker

Because, ultimately, any business, large or small, begins as the visionary journey of one courageous individual who wants to go it alone and start a new business.

The distinction between the ladder world and the entrepreneurial world is not always clear-cut, and some categories of entrepreneur will fall through the net of our definition. For example, how do we define a hospital surgeon who also has a private practice, or a university professor who also runs a private research institute?

But our mainstream definition of entrepreneurs as those who start their own business will fit most people. If you work in the ladder world and you aspire to be your own boss, you fit our definition of aspiring entrepreneur.

Chapter 3

The Ladder-World

We have defined entrepreneur. Now let's define the other side of the coin: ladders.

Most of you will be familiar with the concept of climbing the career ladder. Almost everyone spends time in salaried employment, where a lot of energy is spent in looking constantly upwards to the next rung on the promotional ladder.

Throughout the book, we will use terms like ladder-world, ladder-people, ladder-speak and ladder-think to describe the world of employment. The world of hierarchical structures. The world where regular salaries define the relationship between you and your place of work.

The ladder-world as we know it today is a relatively new phenomenon. Entrepreneurs, on the other hand, have been around since the dawn of civilisation. Long before the ladder era, tradesmen and artisans were embarking on their own business ventures. In biblical times, we were farmers, merchants, fishermen, carpenters, stone-masons, healers, boat-builders, weavers, innkeepers, scribes, potters, bakers, spinners, tanners and goldsmiths.

We learned a trade and sold our expertise or the fruits of our labour. We were entrepreneurs.

The Bible contains precious few references to executive secretaries, divisional heads, junior executives or engineering foremen. Of course, there were also people employed by or coerced into government bureaucracies in ancient times, but most people were their own boss.

The ladder-world came into its own starting about 200 years ago with the industrial revolution. This reached its zenith in the 1950s and 1960s, when ladder-think was encapsulated in the famous catch phrase:

> *"What's good for General Motors is good for the USA, and what's good for the USA is good for General Motors."*

The corporate culture of the ladder-world started to dominate western capitalist thinking. Working on a ladder was considered the norm. Taking its lead from the USA but spreading rapidly to other modern societies, the culture of corporate conformity defined the way you dressed, the people you mingled with, and where you took your vacations.

This same corporate culture made IBM executives look as if they all emerged from the same production line, with their white shirts and blue suits.

(Brian): "You are all individuals"
(Crowd): "We are all individuals".
(Lone voice from the back): "I'm not!"

— *From* Life of Brian

There was a clear and powerful message: don't mess with the ladder world. According to the corporate mentality, the only serious business is big business. The only real players in the business world are the major corporations.

By implication, smaller fry aren't the main story. There was an assumption in the business world that as corporations got bigger and bigger, the justification for small businesses would disappear.

This attitude is still around. There are still many mega-organisations that regard even the smallest entrepreneur as a threat. Close to our (entrepreneurial) home, major corporations continue to flex their muscles against much smaller businesses, as our Case Study shows.

Case Study

Entrepreneur Media is the publisher of Entrepreneur Magazine, *a highly successful publication in the States that has been a great source of inspiration to many an entrepreneur. Entrepreneur Media is engaged in an ongoing legal battle to stop other businesses from using the word "entrepreneur".*

The company has sued over a dozen companies and websites, and one court awarded Entrepreneur Media over €250,000 damages against a PR company that called itself EntrepreneurPR. (I hope I'm not sued by the Ladder Rights Movement for using the word ladder without permission!)

The irony of this situation is that Entrepreneur Media is even suing successful small businesses featured in the magazine! Entrepreneur Magazine *ran an article on Stardock, and then sued them for selling a computer game called Entrepreneur. Stardock's CEO said that the whole thing reminded him of a scene in the movie Independence Day. The President asks the alien: "What do you want us to do?" The alien replies: "Die".*

If Entrepreneur Media succeed in their campaign to stamp out all smaller competitors with the temerity to use the word entrepreneur, what will happen to the hundreds if not thousands of book titles containing the word "entrepreneur" and the countless websites with "entrepreneur" in their domain names? The mind boggles.

Predictions that only big businesses would survive have been proved wrong. Today, the ladder-world itself is encouraging entrepreneurial-style enterprise and initiative within its ranks.

The ladder-world is belatedly recognising what economists and business experts have been saying for years — that a healthy economy is one where more and more entrepreneurs are setting up their own business.

Every year, the Global Enterprise Monitor report urges all governments committed to boosting economic well-being to encourage the entrepreneurial dynamic.

The ladder-world is no longer the only business model around, and many people no longer regard ladders as their natural habitat.

But if you're no longer comfortable on a ladder, where do you go?

The obvious destination is that you leave the ladder-world and embrace the entrepreneurial-world. Many people will identify with the words of Kate Beasedale, the former nurse who eventually became head of Sinclair Montrose Healthcare:

> *"I don't think I've ever been very comfortable working within an organisation. I don't think I was cut out to bide my time and work my way up the ladder, so I began to look for an opportunity to be my own boss."*

In the following chapters, we will examine the implications of the decision to jump off the ladder.

I first started using the ladder as a shorthand symbol for the world of employment in my early entrepreneurial workshops. Participants of all ages seemed to identify with the ladder symbol, so now I bring a real ladder to the workshops as a visual symbolisation of leaving paid employment in the ladder-world.

Case Study

Paul was a workshop participant in his fifties. He had got it into his head that he wanted to give up his day job as a middle manager in an electronics company, and to use his woodworking talents to build and sell fancy dog kennels. After doing some market research and attending a Start Your Own Business course, he left his job and was on the verge of launching his business.

Out of the blue, he received a fabulous offer from another electronics plant. They offered him a huge salary increase, almost total autonomy, his own team, a great pension, the works. He was sorely tempted, and was grappling with what to do.

It was in this very confused state that Paul attended my workshop, with its usual discussion of the ladder-world. At the end of the workshop, he told us of the offer he had just received, and the quandary he was in. The Paul added:

"It was only when I watched you climbing up and down that ladder, and heard you describe how one felt on it and off it, that I realised that I am far more scared of getting back on a ladder again than I am of starting my own business."

He resisted the temptation to take the ladder job, his kennel business is now thriving, and he has branched out into garden sheds and — would you believe it — ladders.

Chapter 4

Is Entrepreneurship Genetically Predetermined?

How much is our decision to work on a ladder or to start our own business influenced by our parents?

Can we learn to be entrepreneurs? Or are we genetically predisposed to become entrepreneurs?

Or is it maybe financial help from our parents that is the key to entrepreneurial success?

A 15-year study of a large group of young American men and their mothers and fathers confirmed that parents' deep pockets (plus the young men's own personal financial assets) had a statistically significant effect on the likelihood that the sons would become self-employed.

But the study identified a far more significant variable: the influence of the employment status of the parents, especially the fathers. The study showed that, although sons of self-employed fathers might choose different occupations, they showed a strong tendency to follow their fathers' footsteps and become self-employed.

In other words, it is not the parents' **financial** capital but their **human** capital — as role models and importers of management skills — that most influences the likelihood of the next generation becoming entrepreneurs.

Several studies have examined the differences between children raised in a home with one or both self-employed parents (non-ladder children), and children whose parents work in corporate or civil service jobs (ladder children).

One such study was led by Professor Dan Miller of Brunel University. He divided the world into Entrepreneurs and Bureaucrats. According to this theory, entrepreneurial parents tend to have entrepreneurial children, because these children absorb the cultural norms of their independent, entrepreneurial parents.

Homes where "business" and "being your own boss" have positive associations are likely to foster an inclination among the children to go it alone.

The home environment of Bureaucratic (ladder) families, on the other hand, does not inspire or encourage children to seek independent non-ladder jobs. Children in ladder families were more likely to emulate the example of their employee parents.

Professor Miller pointed to some of the intangibles we learn at home. For example, a child sitting in the car with his entrepreneurial father will hear all about the problems that employees can cause. This child might learn to regard ladder folk as dull, uninteresting and troublemakers.

A ladder child sitting in the car with her PA mother will hear all about the iniquities of bosses. This child might learn to disparage the notion of entrepreneurship: profit, success, and excess industriousness.

This difference in learned attitudes extends beyond the work environment. It also includes financial and moral issues. Many entrepreneurial children pick up from their parents that it is a badge of honour to try and deprive the taxman of as much money as possible. These same children though, feel very strongly about anyone caught with his hand in their own till.

A ladder child might learn that it's OK to make phone calls on the company's time and at the company's expense, but there's nothing to be done about taxes.

I remember sitting in the lecture hall listening to Professor Miller expounding his views. The theory makes sense, I said to myself at the time, but what he was saying did not fit my personal experience.

My father had hated every minute of his early years as an employee. He fled from the ladder world at the first opportunity, and vowed never to return (a vow he kept). He jumped at the chance to start his own business, and had been his own boss since I was six years old. The whole household revolved around his retail food service business. He was a classic small business owner/manager — always bringing work home, working long hours, quietly worrying about his business, and seeking opportunities for expansion.

According to Miller's Bureaucrat/Entrepreneur theory, I was prime entrepreneur material. I should have absorbed a large dollop of entrepreneurial stimuli at home.

I should have espoused entrepreneurial values. I should have developed an entrepreneurial mindset. I should have resolved from an early age to start my own business.

But I did none of these things. The last thing I thought I wanted to do was be my own boss. There I was, aged 20, studying for my first degree, pondering which career path to take — and the thought of starting my own business had never crossed my mind.

I believed that I lacked the entrepreneurial spirit that seemed to drive my father. As far as I was concerned, the whole thing was a non-starter, a non-issue. My sights were firmly set on joining the ladder-world like everyone around me.

My sense that the entrepreneurial spirit had passed me by was further reinforced when I learned that, according to research, oldest children (like me) are more likely than younger children to start their own businesses. Having to look after younger siblings can generate in the oldest child a sense of autonomy, self-reliance and empowerment — all essential components in the nurturing of the entrepreneurial spirit.

And because parents relate differently to their first child, the latter often displays a heightened sense of responsibility, and is more inclined to absorb family values — including entrepreneurship — than younger siblings.

Well, I was the eldest. Miller had now dealt me a double whammy. In his opinion, I had all the prerequisites to be the entrepreneur I had no intention of becoming. As we will see in the next chapter, in my particular case, Miller was to be proved right.

And while Miller isn't the only theory in town, it was a useful yardstick against which to measure my personal progress towards starting my own business.

There are other theories about the parental role. According to one prominent expert, the mother in particular plays a most powerful role in establishing entrepreneurial action in the male child.

Ultimately, there is no definitive answer to the question of predisposition. There does seem to be a strong statistical likelihood that entrepreneurial families will produce entrepreneurs, and that ladder parents will produce ladder children.

But it doesn't always work out that way. Ladder children can — and do — become entrepreneurs, and entrepreneurial children can — and do — become employees.

In this book, we are restricting ourselves to examining those people who leave the ladder-world to become entrepreneurs. Since most of us spend time in the ladder-world, those of us who want to adopt an entrepreneurial way of life will have to learn a new way of looking at the world.

Ladder children who become entrepreneurs will have to unlearn some of the attitudes they heard at home.

They will have to change their learned reactions to bosses, for a start, since they intend to become one. Children from the ladder-world will need some kind of deprogramming that weans them away from ladder-think.

Entrepreneurial children often start out their working career on a ladder. So even if they absorbed entrepreneurial values at home, and even if they are destined eventually to become entrepreneurs, in the meantime they become temporary ladder-people.

They too will need to unlearn ladder-think as they move to the non-ladder-world.

Chapter 5

Warning: Ladders Can Be Hazardous to Your Health

Why do we need education?

Why do we go to school, college or university?

Why do we seek qualifications?

The real (as opposed to the wishful thinking) answer is:

To get a good job.

There is huge pressure from society in general, and from parents in particular, to land a good job. A safe job. A job with prospects. A job with a pension.

Society defines a good job as going to work for somebody. Joining a company or an organisation. Becoming part of the ladder-world.

And indeed, most of us set out on this route. We accept the societal definition of getting a good job. We study, we get our qualifications, and we get ready to enter the job market.

First, we prepare a CV that's a creative balance between our lack of demonstrable experience and our wish to make a good impression.

Let's say that our job quest is successful. We are offered a job, and we accept. The big day comes, and — feeling very privileged — we turn up for our first day at work. Whatever type of ladder we work for — big or small, commercial or public, online or offline — there's a single common denominator: we are working for someone else.

It is this someone else who pays the bills, and it is this someone else who makes the decisions that affect our work, our job and our earnings.

However much we devote ourselves to our work, however loyal we are to our boss, and however much satisfaction the job gives us, at the end of the day the business is not ours.

Many people reading these words will say: "So what? What's so remarkable about that? What's wrong with loyalty and job satisfaction?"

And of course the answer is: there's absolutely nothing wrong — if that's what you want.

To anyone who is happy to be a ladder-person and to advance up a career ladder, I say "Good luck". Don't think about changing who you are or what you do. And don't let books on entrepreneurship put you off from continuing along the path you have chosen.

There is nothing to apologise for if you inhabit the ladder-world. To quote my son (an entrepreneur himself), "Some of my best friends are ladder people."

Working for a ladder-employer is an honourable occupation. The security of paid employment is very important for many, many people and their families.

The prospect of moving up the career ladder and eventually reaching lucrative and powerful senior positions in the company can be a strong long-term stimulus for many people. I would never urge anyone to jump off the ladder just because others are doing it. No one should leave the ladder-world unless they are sure that this is what they want to do.

But what about people for whom the ladder-world is not OK? What about people who realise that the ladder route is not for them, people who hear an internal voice telling them that there is an alternative to the ladder-world? What about people who spend years accepting the rules and expectations of the ladder-world, only to reach the sad conclusion that they don't really like it there?

Some lucky people have always known that they were entrepreneurs. They have never experienced any doubt, and they have always been obsessed with the idea of being their own boss.

For others, it may be a more gradual process of realisation. It may take longer for them to conclude that, unless and until they work for themselves, they are doomed to a life of frustration.

There's a medical term for people like that. We diagnose them as suffering from the dreaded Entrepreneurial Virus. And just like a computer virus, once it attacks the system, it can cause havoc. It gets into the blood-stream, leaving a person different than before.

Once the entrepreneurial bug enters your soul, you ignore it at your peril. If you don't do anything about it, you'll be asking "What if . . .?" for the rest of your life.

> *"The risk of failure is preferable to enduring a recurring coulda, woulda, shoulda nightmare."*
>
> *— Andy Kessler*

Allow me to share with you how I caught the entrepreneurial bug. I mentioned earlier that, despite my entrepreneurial pedigree, I did not regard myself as entrepreneurial material. After completing my first and second degrees (everyone told me that a BA wasn't enough, I'd need an MA if I really wanted to go places in the ladder-world), I proceeded to climb a succession of ladders.

My entry-level job was on the lowest rung of a ladder — a lowly researcher. On my next ladder, I was still on a lowish rung, but with a more prestigious sounding title: management consultant. On another ladder, I was near the top, with the imposing sounding title of Deputy Managing Director of a small electronics company.

On every ladder, I was competent. I did what I was paid to do. I delivered the goods, so to speak. On a personal level, I was gratified to know that I could perform at managerial level.

A MISMATCH BETWEEN PERFORMANCE AND SOUL

But something was missing. Something wasn't right. To put it bluntly, I wasn't happy in my ladder jobs.

It took me a long time to acknowledge that I wasn't having fun. But there again, who said that work has to be fun? I did not feel a great sense of personal achievement — but who had promised me any such thing?

It's not that I was permanently miserable working on a ladder. There were certainly moments of exhilaration, of triumph, of success, of praise from superiors and peers.

But in the pit of my stomach, I knew there was something wrong. I had a nagging feeling that this wasn't what I wanted. I was aware of a growing mismatch between my performance and my soul.

"Never continue in a job you don't enjoy."

— Rodan of Alexandria

Case Study

Halfway through my ladder career, I went to my father to ask his advice about moving from one ladder to another.

His response puzzled me: "What are the prospects of you taking over the company you work in at present?" What sort of dumb question was that, I thought, and what has this to do with whether or not I should change jobs?

Although I did not understand it at the time, my father was speaking non-ladder talk. In his entrepreneurial world, it was logical that everyone should aspire to own their own company. In his world, if there is no chance of taking over the company you work in, you should move on to a company that does offer such a possibility. His advice to me was strongly grounded in the entrepreneurial values he espoused.

This was a classic case of clashing mindsets. I asked him a question in ladder-speak, he answered in entrepreneur-speak. As a ladder-person (or so I thought at the time), having a stake in the business was not an issue. I did not even regard myself as particularly ambitious.

Incidentally, I took my father's advice to move company, but not for the reasons he put forward. It was only years later that I realised where he was coming from.

Eventually, after I had plodded my way through several ladder jobs, the penny dropped. At the age of 30, after several years of gainful ladder-employment, I realised that I didn't actually like ladders after all.

In fact, I had developed a positive aversion to ladders. I had reached the inescapable conclusion that ladder-life was not for me.

> *"I'm a bad employee and need to build my own castles in the air."*
>
> — Richard Koch

I discovered an awful — and awesome — truth about myself: I was a bad employee, constitutionally unfit to work under any boss.

I realised that, in every employment situation, I inevitably found that my boss was an ignoramus (in my entrepreneurial workshops, I use stronger language). By definition, none of my bosses ever appreciated my talents.

The questions I found myself asking are the questions anyone contemplating moving off the ladder must ask:

- What has changed?
- Why am I no longer satisfied with climbing up the corporate ladder?
- Why is the esteem of my bosses and my peers no longer enough?
- What has precipitated the conversion from ladder-person to non-ladder-person?

- Why do I now believe that I would be happier on my own than on someone else's ladder?

- Why do I fear that staying on the ladder is detrimental to my well-being?

Some people who ask themselves these questions in fact remain in the ladder-world for all their working lives. They may be frustrated, cursing their lot in life, but they stay.

Why? Because, as anyone who has ever tried to lose weight or give up smoking will tell you, **wanting** isn't enough.

You've got to make the next critical jump. You've got to actually make the move into the non-ladder-world.

"I'd rather be my own general than a loyal corporate foot soldier."

— Michael Bloomberg

Chapter 6

What Triggers Can Push You Off the Ladder?

Not everyone knows instinctively that they were destined to become their own boss. Some people's entrepreneurial instincts are triggered or awakened by a traumatic termination of employment, feelings of dissatisfaction, or a flash of inspiration as an opportunity is spotted.

In this chapter, we look at some of the triggers that can push people off the ladder.

GETTING FIRED

You're an expert in your field. You have spent your entire professional life working for a major multinational. You always believed that job security in this blue chip company was guaranteed. Then one day you're history.

Whatever your particular scenario, getting the sack can be a powerful motivation for becoming an entrepreneur. When you've been pushed off the ladder, choosing self-employment can be as much an act of liberation as an act of desperation.

Case Study

Raymond was a computer teacher. He was always in trouble with the school management, and he kept threatening to quit. One day, the principal of the school called his bluff, and Raymond found himself out of the job he had held for 20 years.

His educational supervisor, with whom he had enjoyed a warm personal relationship, came to visit him a few days later. Whatever state he expected Raymond to be in, the supervisor was not prepared for the effusive welcome he received.

"Hallelujah!" said Raymond. "This was exactly the push I needed. I haven't been happier in years. And you'll never believe what I did yesterday: I opened my own computing business."

Is getting fired the excuse you think you've been waiting for? If you have been dreaming, scheming and planning for this moment, maybe getting fired is the right trigger for doing something about starting your own business.

If getting the sack came like a bolt out of the blue, the first thing you experience is a severe blow to your ego. Beware of a knee-jerk reaction that sends you into the arms of entrepreneurship before you have had time to think about it and analyse your feelings. To draw an analogy from a relationship breaking down, beware of the rebound.

Whatever the circumstances, there is an important question you must ask yourself when you find yourself jobless: were you fired because you don't fit **this** ladder, or because you don't fit **any** ladder?

There's a big difference.

If the root cause of getting the sack is a personality clash with your superior or your boss, you may fare better with a more enlightened boss on a different ladder. Not sure? Test it out. Entrepreneurship is not an automatic solution for everyone who gets fired.

It's a different story if you believe that getting the sack was inevitable. For example, if you took paid employment even though you felt in your bones that you were not ladder material, you may well end up fighting with any and every boss. You probably never last long in paid jobs, and you'll never really be happy in paid employment.

Most people don't automatically think of becoming an entrepreneur when they are fired for the first or even the second time. But if it becomes a habit, it's time to look at an alternative. Maybe the time has come to work for no one but yourself. Because by now, you are basically unemployable. You're going to have to ditch the ladder world and go it alone.

DISILLUSIONMENT

Corporate culture means guidelines, rules and manifestos. This is how corporations try to handle thousands of individuals, each with their own agenda and their own requirements.

Impatience with the rules is often the first signal of entrepreneurial stirrings in employees who eventually leave to start their own business.

Disillusionment at work can begin with an ill-defined uneasiness. You know something isn't right, but you can't put your finger on it. You are not exactly unhappy at work, but you're aware that you're not really feeling fulfilled.

You're good at what you do, but you're not sure you're doing what you want. You get on OK with your work colleagues, but you wonder if there isn't something better out there. You accept the authority of your boss, but you don't necessarily respect his or her judgement.

Sometimes, something more specific can trigger disillusionment. Seeing colleagues with less experience than you being promoted over your head can be disillusioning. The realisation that playing politics rather than original thought and initiative can determine your promotion prospects can be a sad and disheartening experience.

As with getting the sack, you must ask yourself whether your disillusionment is with this particular ladder or with all ladders. If there's a chance that you could still find your comfort zone on another ladder, test the theory before rushing off to open your own business.

FRUSTRATION

Frustration can be both a trigger and a root cause of wanting to become an entrepreneur. Sometimes you look at your work situation, and you realise that you want to be the one in charge.

It's not a big jump from "I know I can do things better, if only they'd listen to me" to "I want to make my own decisions, and be responsible for the consequences".

If left unattended, your frustration will fester. You will start resenting your boss, and then your colleagues.

The trick is to realise that **they** are not the problem. **You are**. Your boss and your colleagues, like many ladder-people, might be quite contented where they are. They see nothing wrong with the way they do things. You are the one with ants in your pants, not them.

So if the frustration gets too much to bear, and you recall similar feelings in previous places of work, maybe it's time to get off the ladder and start your own business.

SEEING AN OPPORTUNITY

Sometimes the trigger for wanting to leave the safe haven of the ladder-world is a business opportunity that seems too good to miss.

Opportunities are everywhere, but it takes a special talent to spot their potential. Ladder-people and entrepreneurs look at the same reality and see different things. Entrepreneurs can almost smell an opportunity.

But without a predisposition to an entrepreneurial perspective, it is rare for ladder-people to even consider following up the most lucrative or promising opportunity.

"Opportunities are usually disguised as hard work, so most people don't recognise them."

— Ann Landers

Case Study

Victoria and Amy both work in the office of a large agricultural enterprise. Because both girls have language skills, they have the task of negotiating with contractors in Eastern Europe to supply them with farmhands. The girls soon master the intricacies of the bureaucracy, and can now get farmhands within days instead of waiting for weeks and sometimes months.

The girls hear from talk in the town that other farms are having great difficulty finding farmhands. A light goes on in Victoria's head. Here's a real business opportunity. With her specialised expertise, she could help several farmers find farmhands faster. She has always had a secret wish to run her own business, and now she sees a way of achieving her dream.

All excited, Victoria goes to Amy to share her idea. Amy listens, and within seconds she is busy deflating Victoria's idea. Where will you find the labourers? Where will you find the farmers? What will your boyfriend say? What makes you think you can do it?

> *Remember, Amy sits in the same office as Victoria. She is exposed to the same information. But where Victoria sees an opportunity to create her own business, Amy sees only problems. Where Victoria sees a chance to follow her dream, Amy clings to the stability and security of their ladder.*

MONEY TO SPARE

There is another kind of opportunity that needs addressing: money. Circumstances can suddenly land a confirmed ladder-person with a sizeable amount of money. The lottery. A bequest. A huge handout when you retired. A killing on the markets.

Be warned: having money to play with may be a very unsound basis for deciding that now is the time to be your own boss. Entrepreneurship is about vitality and enthusiasm, not just about money. You've got to be driven by a dream, not just pulled along by a money pot.

> ### Case Study
>
> *Johnny could not believe his luck. He'd married into a very wealthy family, with oodles of money. They had a huge house, they took trips and cruises, and the children went to the best private schools. He was made.*

Johnny himself came from a ladder family. His father had worked in the same company all his working life, rising to chief buyer. Johnny had studied economics, gone on to get his doctorate, and was a university lecturer when he married.

At first, he worked in the research department of his father-in-law's electrical goods empire. But Johnny wasn't happy. The thought of all that money around was getting to him.

After nagging his pappy-in-law, Johnny joined the company's investment department. He proved quite adept at the job, and was soon handling sizeable sums of money. But he still wanted more, and he persuaded his rather reluctant father-in-law to give him a couple of million in order to set up his own portfolio management company.

Johnny was overjoyed. "I'm an entrepreneur at last", he told everyone. He should have said, "I'm an entrepreneur who won't last", because within six months he had lost it all. He had fallen in love with the idea of being his own boss, but he really had no idea what it involved. He had never had to work hard in his life, and didn't see why he should start now.

He had never been responsible for his own finances, so he embarked on an orgy of spending. He had plush offices and a staff of four before he even had a single client.

Johnny should never have become an entrepreneur. The opportunity that triggered his decision was about money, not about a genuine entrepreneurial urge.

In this chapter, we looked at some of the triggers that can push you off the ladder. Many people leave a job without any clear idea of what to do next except for the determination to somehow start a new business. In the following chapter, we look at how we decide what to do next.

Chapter 7

What Do You Want to be When You Grow Up?

You've reached the conclusion that you must leave the ladder-world. But deciding to leave is one thing. Knowing what to do when you leave is another.

This was the dilemma I faced. After years of ladder-hopping, I was at the end of my tether. I knew that, for health reasons, I had to avoid ladders. There had also been a powerful trigger — the last ladder job I held ended with an ignominious dismissal three days before I would have become permanent.

It felt more like relief than courage when I swore that I would never work for anyone again. But deciding what business to set up was far more difficult.

To resolve my dilemma, I sat down at my kitchen table with a blank piece of paper. One column was for the activities I felt I was *skilled* at doing; the second column was for things that I really *enjoyed* doing.

At first, the skills list looked easy. But if you are looking for skills that could form the basis of a new business, you have to think very carefully. My MA had been in industrial sociology, but I had never worked as an industrial sociologist. I could manage departments and people, but were these skills to a business on?

Finally, I found a skill. Because I was living in Israel at the time, and because I was fluent in both English and Hebrew, I wrote down: "Bi-lingual".

The second column was much harder. "What do I enjoy doing?" I realised that this was not really part of my vocabulary. As a good and obedient child who did what he was told, I had a keen sense of responsibility. I understood the language of "I must".

> *"I daresay one profits more by the mistakes one makes off one's own bat than by doing the right thing on somebody' else's advice".*
>
> — Somerset Maugham

But, because I had nearly always followed solicited and unsolicited advice from my elders and betters, I was unfamiliar with the language of "I want".

One thing was clear. You can't start your own business unless you know what you want. This was a moment of truth. It was time to burrow deeper into my feelings, and to ask myself what I wanted to be when I grow up?

There was one word that popped into my head, a word whose name I almost dared not speak: creativity. I knew that, since childhood, I had felt creative urges, but I was scared to acknowledge my creativity.

It didn't take an Einstein (or a Freud) to see where this mental block came from. Two of my teachers at boarding school had taken it upon themselves to offer wise advice before I embarked on life after high school. I can still hear their words ringing in my ears.

"You're a good B" said one teacher. In plain English: don't have ideas above your abilities. You are not A material, but you're also no dunce. "Don't try for Oxford or Cambridge Universities", he added, "Go to a good redbrick university". Always the obedient student, I duly obliged. I got a B in every matriculation subject, I didn't even try for Oxbridge, and I got a B in my BA. Talk about a self-fulfilling prophecy.

The other teacher was equally well-meaning, and equally misguided. "Whatever you do, don't write — you lack imagination", she told me. And I believed her. She was a teacher, after all, and teachers know best. Thanks to her constructive advice, I did not put creative pen to paper for the next 10 years.

Hardly surprising that any thought of creativity always conjured up memories of my teachers' admonitions.

Self-fulfilling Prophecies

Most people I know can recount horror stories about receiving disastrous career advice from teachers.

There is a phenomenon in educational theory called the Pygmalion Effect. According to Greek mythology, King Pygmalion of Cyprus carved a statue of a perfect woman. He wanted his creation to come to life. He believed that, by willing this perfect woman to come alive, with a bit of help from the goddess Venus, she would indeed come alive. The Pygmalion Effect in education is the phenomenon where a persistently-held belief in another person's abilities becomes a reality.

In other words, belief in potential creates potential. Tell a teacher that a pupil is bright, and the teacher will be more supportive. Tell a teacher that a pupil is a troublemaker, and the teacher will have expectations of such behaviour — and treat the pupil accordingly.

The trouble is that self-fulfilling prophecies can also affect and distort an impressionable pupil's self-perception. Such pupils will internalise the teacher's opinion about their potential, and will find themselves living up to teachers' expectations. That is fine if the teacher's expectations are higher than the pupils' own expectations. But if they are lower, the teacher has done the pupil no favours in life.

Back at my kitchen table, I now had "Bi-lingual" in the skills column and "Creativity" in the I Want column. I spent several days wondering how to merge these columns to create a viable business.

> *"Destiny is not a matter of chance, it is a matter of choice. It is not a thing to be waited for, it is a thing to be achieved."*
>
> — William Jenning Bryan

At this point, one of those chance encounters occurred that helped put the pieces of the entrepreneurial puzzle into place.

An Israeli friend asked me as a favour to write the English text for a small brochure on a car alarm system he had developed. Without a second thought, I wrote the text, and even drew a rough sketch of how the text should be laid out. He thanked me.

A week later, my friend called to tell me that his graphic designer wanted to meet me. "What's a graphic designer?" I asked defensively, "and why does he want to meet me?"

"He's the guy who designs and produces brochures," replied my friend. "After he saw your text, he wants you to write texts for other clients he's handling."

Bingo! Here was a niche market that uniquely suited my skills. Here was something I could do. Here was something I'd love to do.

Anyone who wants to get off the ladder and set up a business has to find a match between "I can" and "I want". When you find the magic combination, you're ready for lift-off.

Belatedly, I realised that all the things I had ever enjoyed doing were creative pursuits. Sketching. The puppet theatre shows I used to give. Scripts for school revues. The roles I used to play on stage. The intricate models I built with the huge Lego set I bought for my oldest son the day he was born, on the pretext that I had to practice until he was old enough to enjoy it.

More bits of the puzzle fell into place. I had a life-long fascination with words. I'd been an avid Scrabble player since I was 8. I loved puns. I loved word games. I had always devoured anything in print, from the small print on the cereal packet to the ads in the paper.

When I assembled all the pieces, I finally saw a way of matching my language skills, my creativity and my love of words. I would write English advertising, marketing and promotional texts for a non-English speaking market. I would become a freelance copywriter (which was a new word for me.) After all, I already had one client, the graphic designer. How hard could it be, I asked myself, to find more clients who appreciated my skills?

So I commandeered half the kitchen table, and bought myself a second-hand electric typewriter, some paper and a couple of pens. I created a company name, bought myself some Letraset (remember what that is?) to create a logo, and had business cards printed.

Feeling a bit of a fraud, with a pathetically naïve ignorance of what I was doing, yet driven by a confidence I never knew I possessed, I found myself in business.

Almost 15 years after leaving school, I had finally discovered what I wanted to be when I grow up.

And here I am, over 20 years later, still writing brochures, websites and newsletters for clients all over the world. And still loving it!

Everyone has their own route to the magic moment of truth. The realisation that you are destined to be an entrepreneur can hit you at any age. But the process is the same. First comes the realisation that you must leave the ladder world. Then comes the choice of an area of expertise that you make your own.

It is not always immediately apparent in what field you can excel, in what business you can make your mark. Opinion is divided as to whether you should choose to work in a niche market or in a market with plenty of competitors. Personally, I gravitated towards a niche market, but this must be a personal choice.

Once this critical decision has been made, the fun can really begin.

> *"Choose a job you love, and you will never have to work a day in your life."*
>
> — Confucius

Chapter 8

Fire in Your Belly and Nine Other Prerequisites for Being Your Own Boss

Do you need particular personality or character traits to decide to become your own boss?

Opinions differ. Some people claim that there is no such thing as a definable predisposition to entrepreneurship, and that it is impossible to say that entrepreneurs are all this or all that.

While I accept that we shouldn't put all entrepreneurs into a definitional straightjacket, I also believe that you need a healthy mix of specific traits if you're going to find the courage to get off the ladder and go it alone.

In this chapter, we examine some of the prerequisites for becoming an entrepreneur, some of the personality traits that help us identify the entrepreneur. There's always a danger with such lists that they end up sounding like horoscopes (or like the self-assessment tests I poked fun at earlier.)

This is not an exhaustive list, and should not be taken too literally — but it will be a useful guide for defining the ballpark in which entrepreneurs play.

1. INDEPENDENCE

Entrepreneurs have a strong independent streak. Their need for freedom is what defines them. They can be very stubborn, and they don't like being told what to do.

Entrepreneurs are participants, not observers. They tend to be driven and focused, and they have the self-confidence to follow their own vision. Entrepreneurs don't understand why they shouldn't do something that hasn't been done before. They have a huge belief in themselves and in what they are trying to create.

> *"Self-confidence is only useful when you put it to work."*
>
> — Anonymous

When in doubt, they will do something themselves rather than rely on anyone else. They are notoriously intolerant of ineptitude, and can be quite crusty if things aren't done exactly to their liking. Many entrepreneurs struggle to fit into society, believing that no one — especially the ladder world — understands them properly.

For many entrepreneurs, independence is a physical as well as a mental state. They need — and value — their physical space. I knew a graphic designer who boldly placed the following sign in his studio:

Hourly rate:	€65 per hour
You watch:	€100 per hour
You help:	€150 per hour

2. TENACITY

When entrepreneurs get a bee in their bonnet, watch out! In the pursuit of their goals, they can be stubborn to the point of pig-headedness. They act decisively, and don't waste time wondering whether they did the right thing. They are disciplined and focused, and attack any job to be done with persistence and tenacity.

Entrepreneurs don't sit around waiting for things to happen. They get their act together, and beaver away at the job to be done. They are impatient with slovenly work and lackadaisical attitudes, and they do not suffer fools lightly.

Entrepreneurs are high on life, and often resent having to "waste" part of their life on sleep. And even the time they devote to sleep is filled with new ideas on how to fix a problem that's been bugging them. (While I was working on this book, I used to dream that I was being pursued by some of the characters from the Case Studies.)

"He who wants milk should not sit himself in the middle of a pasture waiting for a cow to back up to him."

— Anonymous

Case Study

Sue worked for years as a highly-paid and highly-valued software programmer with a number of companies. She enjoyed her work, but she was not always enthralled with her workplaces.

Once she had accumulated enough capital, she left the ladder-world to follow up an idea that had been keeping her awake at nights: a new system for preventing credit card fraud.

Every time she thought she'd cracked the problem, a new one arose. Six months passed, and she had nothing tangible to show for her efforts. Another six months passed, and her capital was running out. She raised a second mortgage to give herself breathing space. "I know the solution is out there, and I'm determined to find it", she kept repeating to herself.

Nothing could dissuade Sue from her course. Her friends and family begged her to give up. Nothing doing.

One day, it all came together. Commercial success followed almost immediately.

For Sue, it had never been a question of "if" she would succeed, it was always a question of "When".

3. INITIATIVE

Entrepreneurs are doers. They are quick to take the initiative and quick to recognise and seize opportunities. They are proactive, and cannot stand procrastination. They want to get on with things.

Much of this stems from a natural self-confidence and self-reliance.

Scratch most entrepreneurs, and you will find that they used to be adept at finding ways to earn extra pocket-money while they were growing up. Not only because they wanted the extra dough, but because money-making opportunities came along — and they seized the initiative.

At boarding school, I used to earn extra money by typing class work for my classmates, and by shining shoes for lazy sixth-formers. At university, I ran a small grocery supply company to help pay my tuition. (Interestingly, it never occurred to me at the time that this was an entrepreneurial pursuit.)

"Small opportunities are often the start of great enterprises."

— Demosthenes

4. LIVING WITH UNCERTAINTY

People who need a high level of predictability in their lives will rarely risk the uncertainty of starting their own business.

Entrepreneurs are able to live with this uncertainty. They seem to thrive in an unstructured environment, and can probably survive on a level of risk that would make ladder people queasy.

"I am a great believer in luck. I find the harder I work, the more I have of it."

— Stephen Leacock

What others might call foolhardy, entrepreneurs call normal. What other people call luck, entrepreneurs call opportunity.

It's the same with challenges. Situations that can send shivers down the spines of ladder-people also send shivers down the spines of entrepreneurs — except that these are not shivers of fear, they are tingles of excitement!

One of the keys to coping with uncertainty is discipline. Self-discipline, to be precise. Entrepreneurs need the self-discipline to get up early and start working on whatever needs doing. They don't need anyone to chase them.

Case Study

Young marrieds Debbie and Burt were both hired as freelance consultants by the same Internet start-up in London. She had a strong entrepreneurial disposition, and had always worked freelance. He was from firm ladder stock, had just lost his ladder job, and thought this was a good opportunity to work on his own.

Debbie was hired as a technical consultant, Burt as a programmer. They were both told by their start-up client that they were only required to come into the office one day a week, the rest of the work could be done on their computers in their apartment.

Debbie got up each morning, sat at her computer, and hammered away until she had done a day's work. Nothing distracted her — not the street sounds, not the kids in the school playground next door, not the shopping mall down the street.

For Burt, however, "four days working from home" meant four days of sleeping in, running errands, going shopping, and playing pool with his friends. He didn't get it — and was most surprised at the end of the week when he hadn't completed his workload.

He was even more surprised by the attitude of the client, who expected "eight hours worth of work" every day. After a couple of weeks, it was clear that he was not fit for this kind of work, and he left to work for the local library where he thrived.

> *As a ladder-person, Burt could not get used to the non-structured workday or to the self-discipline that comes with being an entrepreneur.*

> *"He that riseth late, must trot all day, and shall scarce overtake his business at night."*
>
> — Benjamin Franklin

5. OUT OF THE BOX

Entrepreneurs have a tendency to think outside of the box. They see the extraordinary in the ordinary, they think innovatively and laterally, and they allow their imagination to take them on fascinating journeys.

> *"Imagination is more important than knowledge."*
>
> — Albert Einstein

Many entrepreneurs nurture their out-of-the-box thinking by keeping whimsical articles in their workspace - both as an inspiration and as a way of reminding them not to take themselves too seriously.

At the Epcot Centre in Florida about 15 years ago, I was inspired by my visit to the Kodak Pavilion of Imagination. As I was leaving, I bought a fluffy souvenir toy. Ever since then, Figment has sat opposite me as I pound the keys.

I have a colleague who has a sign in front of him with a little dot in the middle. The caption reads: "This is the point that I stare at when I concentrate".

Entrepreneurs are prepared to bend the rules, to be different. They are great believers in listening to their instincts. For entrepreneurs, just because no one ever did it before doesn't mean it's not a good idea. On the contrary, they are often spurred on to try solutions that no one else believes will work.

6. MAKING SACRIFICES

Entrepreneurs are willing to make sacrifices, to adopt a long view of things. They are prepared to forego some of the fun and the luxuries until such time that they can enjoy it — what is known as delayed gratification.

Entrepreneurs know that their lives are different from what others consider "normal". They don't go out to lunch with everybody else — very often they don't go out to lunch at all.

Entrepreneurs are quite happy to work early in the morning before the rest of the working world, and work into the night if there's a deadline to be met.

Entrepreneurs themselves don't see this as "making sacrifices". For them, it's just getting the job done.

7. NOT DEVASTATED BY FAILURE

Some of the most famous entrepreneurs in history had a string of failures before they finally made it.

Walt Disney made a loss on his first five business ventures. Donald Trump made millions, lost millions, and made them all back again.

Failure can be an important catalyst of change. You will even hear entrepreneurs expressing how sorry they are for people who have only experienced success, because they don't know the rewards of failure.

Entrepreneurs can live with mistakes because they see a bigger picture. If something goes wrong, they think in terms of how to avoid similar problems next time. Because, in most cases, they are sure there will be a next time. Entrepreneurs are incurable optimists. "I'll get it right next time" is their motto.

Case Study

Geoff made the classic mistake of allowing one client to dominate his ad agency's business.

While he was going through a divorce, the marketing director of the client company — who knew them socially — sided with Geoff's wife, and cancelled his contract with Geoff's agency as a punishment.

Geoff appealed to the client CEO to overturn this unprofessional decision, but to no avail. Geoff saw his turnover decimated overnight. The agency almost went to the wall, but Geoff never thought of quitting.

> He battened down the hatches, released half his staff, regrouped, and vowed never to allow a situation where a single client could account for such a large volume of his business again. He did not permit this major setback to unnerve him, and he survived to tell the tale.

"When I was a young man, I observed that nine out of ten things I did were failures. I didn't want to be a failure, so I did ten times more work."

— George Bernard Shaw

8. CRAZINESS

One hundred and twenty pairs of eyes were focused on the speaker as he walked up to the podium with a decided spring in his step. We had all signed up to a two-year programme for entrepreneurs. This was the opening address on the opening day of the programme. We were anxious to hear what important message the guest speaker had for us.

He stood there, looked up as if surprised to see us there, and said: "I understand that everyone here runs their own business." [Pause.] "Are you mad?" he roared.

We were shocked. Had we come here to be insulted?

"You must be crazy", he continued. "Anyone who leaves the safe haven of the corporate world to open their own business must be bonkers. It's axiomatic."

For the next 30 minutes, John Teeling regaled us with his tales. We were in stitches as he recounted the run-ins he'd had with bankers, lawyers, government officials, and countless other functionaries who had tried to stop him from realising his dream. Teeling is absolutely right. You definitely have to be off-the-wall to want to go it alone. The statistics can be frightening. For every 100 entrepreneurs who opened their new business yesterday, over half will have gone out of business within the next three years.

It's not just the statistics. Just listen to what people all around are telling you. They will tell you that you are mad, crazy, you've lost it, out of your mind, unstable, unbalanced, foolish, stubborn, arrogant. In their terms, you are all of these, and more.

> *"The moon could not go on shining if it paid any attention to the little dogs that bark at it."*

Entrepreneurs see this as all perfectly normal. You see an opportunity. You know you can make it work. You go ahead and do it.

For entrepreneurs, the decision is perfectly rational. They accept that others will regard them as demented, and they go ahead and do it anyway.

9. CHUTZPAH

Entrepreneurs have to have chutzpah — a wonderfully evocative Yiddish word that means nerve, cheek, gall.

You need chutzpah to believe you can make it on your own.

You need chutzpah — and guts — to get off the ladder.

You need chutzpah — and courage — to embark on a new venture with no guarantee that it will succeed.

You need chutzpah to try to compete with established companies in your field.

You need chutzpah to march up to your potential customers with nothing more than a wish and a prayer and convince them that they should buy whatever goods or services you are selling.

Case Study

Within months of launching his import-export operation, Cliff Hardcastle was asked by the old Thorn EMI defence division to supply digital displays. Under the mistaken impression that the Thorn division that made the displays had ceased production, the buyer urgently needed an outside source.

Cliff discovered that the buyer had been misinformed. In fact, the Thorn display plant had simply relocated a couple of hundred miles away. So Cliff went to the plant, obtained a quote for the displays, added 30% to the price, and went back to the buyer at Thorn EMI's defence division who promptly placed a big order.

Thus it was that Cliff sold Thorn its own products. That's chutzpah!

People with chutzpah also believe that the stars are always in their favour. Their rose-tinted spectacles, their gift of the gab, and their belief that nothing is impossible come in very handy when they are trying to persuade (I almost wrote bamboozle) the bank to double the size of the loan they have just approved.

10. FIRE IN YOUR BELLY

Whether you're a born entrepreneur or the entrepreneurial realisation comes more gradually, once you get the idea into your head that you are going to start your own business, you get a fire in your belly.

With fire in your belly, you are invincible.

With fire in your belly, you can turn the zaniest idea into a workable business proposition.

And best of all, this fire in your belly cannot be extinguished by other people throwing cold water on your ideas. Because once the fire in your belly takes over, you're launched into a different stratosphere.

As a new entrepreneur, you can't afford half measures when you start a new business. If you can't give it total commitment, don't bother. If you don't have fire in your belly, it's unlikely to happen.

> *"I can instinctively tell the difference between people who have fire in their belly and those who see their ideas primarily as a way to get rich."*

— Venture capitalist, Arthur Rock

Entrepreneurs are passionate about their business, and it shows.

Entrepreneurs know that they are capable of accomplishing anything they set their mind to. You can almost see the energy bursting out of them. Entrepreneurs are also highly motivated and always enthusiastic. Where others see disaster, they see potential, and when others think it can't be done, they come up with plenty of solutions. They truly believe in what they are doing, and they are constantly re-inventing and fine-tuning.

> *"Enthusiasm, like mumps and measles, is highly contagious."*

— Emory Ward

Entrepreneurs have pride of ownership, the same sort of pride you have for your family, your home or your car. The passion that entrepreneurs feel when they start their own business can be compared to the addition of a new family member.

Chapter 9

Entrepreneurs and Ladder-People — Breeds Apart

In the last chapter, we discussed the personality and character ballpark in which entrepreneurs play. In this chapter, we will examine some of the differences between entrepreneurs and ladder-people.

To borrow and misquote a phrase, Ladder-People are from Mercury, Entrepreneurs are from Jupiter. By this I mean that they are two totally different breeds. Neither breed is superior, but if you are planning to move from the ladder to the entrepreneurial world, you have to understand the differences.

The ladder-world often seems to have a problem making entrepreneurs out. It's as if entrepreneurs are being accused of ill-defined crimes by the ladder establishment.

GUILTY AS CHARGED

In my entrepreneurial workshops, I act out an imaginary courtroom scene that symbolises the conceptual and perceptual chasm that can divide the ladder and the non-ladder worlds.

The entrepreneur is standing in the dock of the Old Bailey. The learned judge looks over his bifocals and tells the accused that, after weighing all the evidence against him, he finds him guilty as charged of independent thought, ambition and initiative.

"Furthermore", says his lordship, "since you have expressed no remorse for your actions, I sentence you to 30 years hard labour as an entrepreneur. Prisoner, have you anything to say?"

"Yes, m'lud," he replies. "When can I start?"

The judge — symbolising the ladder-world — just doesn't understand what makes the entrepreneur tick. What the judge regards as a harsh sentence is regarded by the entrepreneur as a bonus.

Ladder-people often seem to harbour ill-will towards anyone willing to risk their money, and even their homes, to follow a dream.

The very things that turn an entrepreneur on, can have the opposite effect on ladder-people.

Why are the two breeds so often on a collision course? Why does the ladder-world view the entrepreneurial world with such suspicion, incomprehension and often downright hostility?

Maybe envy has something to do with it. Maybe it's a feeling harboured by ladder-people that entrepreneurs are somehow more vital, more alive, more creative.

Many ladder-people accuse entrepreneurs of being "only driven by money". Yet there are so many entrepreneurs for whom the need to be independent has a much higher priority than the need to make money. There are many entrepreneurs who are prepared to forego high earnings for the more prized aphrodisiac of freedom.

We all know of people who gave up steady ladder employment to start their own business — knowing in advance that they were going to earn less than they did on the ladder. Because it's not only about money.

It is difficult to advise entrepreneurs on how to counter negative vibes from the ladder-world. The differences in outlook between the two worlds can be fundamental.

Let's take a look at some of the basic parameters that differentiate ladder-people and entrepreneurs.

1. DIFFERENT ATTITUDE TO TIME

The ladder and non-ladder worlds wear different watches. In the ladder-world, the two most important numerals on the watch are often 9 and 5, and the biggest challenge is to fill the gap between them. On entrepreneurial watches, it often feels like you're trying to squeeze more than 24 hours into the day.

2. DIFFERENT PACE

Entrepreneurs are always in a hurry. There's always something else or something new to be done. Entrepreneurs try to cheat the clock by doing some of tomorrow's work today.

The pace in many ladder organisations can be very different. Their whole attitude to time is different. Urgency is relative, and tomorrow is another day.

3. DIFFERENT CULTURES

It's not just in the workplace that the differences between the ladder and entrepreneurial cultures are apparent. The clash between the two worlds can be loudest in the home, especially if you work from home.

Ladder-people can have a real problem understanding how you can be at work if you're at home. They are not comfortable with entrepreneurial work practices, which they regard as haphazard — sort of unnatural, wrong. For them, home is not for work. If you're home, it means you've got time to run errands, do the shopping, and fix the plastering that fell off the wall.

Entrepreneurs have a hard time convincing their ladder partners that when they are sitting on the sofa at home, with their head tilted backwards and eyes closed, they could be planning the staff vacation schedule, debating whether to buy a new piece of equipment, or worrying how to meet the deadline for an advertising campaign.

4. DIFFERENT PRIORITIES

Entrepreneurs make time fit their schedules. In the ladder-world, employees often want their schedules to fit the clock.

For entrepreneurs, meals and coffee-breaks are totally flexible, and can often be regarded as dispensable luxuries. For ladder-people, meals and coffee-breaks can define the working day.

5. DIFFERENT COMMITMENT

If an entrepreneur is not totally committed to the business, the business fails. Ladder employees can be loyal and dedicated, but ultimately their commitment to their employer falls short of the fanatical variety associated with entrepreneurs.

"Boldness has genius, power and magic in it"

— Goethe

When Goethe wrote about the magic of boldness, he must have had the entrepreneur's commitment in mind. According to Goethe, as soon as you definitely commit yourself, providence moves too. Things start happening to support your decision. Crucial information suddenly comes your way. People too.

6. DIFFERENT WORK ETHIC

When you own your own business, your work ethic knows no bounds. You live and breathe the business, and you sometimes cannot understand anyone who has a different attitude to work.

Case Study

Some years back, as part of my copywriting consultancy work, I spent a couple of days working in a ladder office. I was given a desk, a computer, and a list of jobs to be done. They wanted me there in person (rather than via email) in order to troubleshoot in real-time with their development team.

I suffered genuine culture shock. It had been years since I had sat for a full day in an office, and I had forgotten what office life can be like.

This was a hard-working, smart and committed team, but I had a real problem getting used to their work ethic. I could not believe the eagerness with which they awaited lunch, the amount of discussion over where they were going to eat, and the length of time they actually spent at lunch.

I'm not saying this was wrong. I'm just saying that it brought home to me the different work environments and work norms in the ladder and non-ladder worlds.

---

7. DIFFERENT CONCEPT OF JOB SECURITY

The ladder world represents security for ladder-people. They are comfortable with the fact that their work-life is organised and structured. They need the security of the regular salary.

Entrepreneurs can feel stifled by the same structures that appeal to ladder-people. Entrepreneurs look to themselves to provide security. Naturally, they miss the regular salary, but the price they feel they have to pay in the salary-world is way too high.

Entrepreneurs also know that the job security of a ladder salary can be an illusion. In today's business world, unless you are answering a demand that the market needs, you'll soon be out of a job, whether you work for Microsoft or in your own office.

8. DIFFERENT ATTITUDES TO RISK

Organisations and committees are not natural risk-takers. The ladder-world prefers to work to a more predictable game-plan. Entrepreneurs are stereotyped as risk-takers. Actually, I am not convinced that risk-taking distinguishes entrepreneurs from ladder-people. I think it is the definition of risk that is different.

For many entrepreneurs, going out on a limb, starting a business in a field that no one else has tried, and doing things differently, all have more to do with original and creative thinking than with risk-taking. Many entrepreneurs would define their actions as survival, not as risk.

Chapter 10

Bad Things Can Happen to Nice Entrepreneurs

Moving off the ladder to start your own business can give you a great buzz. Once you make your decision, you will thrive on the excitement. You are borne on a wave of enthusiasm so intense that you are ready to take on all comers.

> *"Work, work, work.*
> *Work, work, work.*
> *Work, work, work."*
>
> — Governor William J Le Potomaine in
> "Blazing Saddles"

But there can be problems too. From every direction. And you're better off knowing about them in advance.

I have paraphrased an anguished reader's letter that I found in a business magazine:

"Why does everyone extol the virtues of working 20 hours a day and getting no sleep?

Why does no one write about the entrepreneur's spouse or partner going crazy (or worse — leaving the relationship) because the entrepreneur is never around?

Why does no one write about the cost to the entrepreneur of not having a social life, not taking vacations, not engaging in any sort of physical exercise?

I never read about an entrepreneur who sacrificed everything, including family, friends, and health, and was truly happy.

I never read the story from the perspective of the spouse, partner, friend, or employee who bears the burden of dealing with irritable, cranky, and evasive entrepreneurs.

Entrepreneurs are in such a hurry to get to "someday" that they never stop to enjoy the moment. They go through years of pain and frustration before they realise that when someday arrives, it won't have been worth it."

There's more than a grain of truth in each of these complaints. Entrepreneurs must somehow find a balance between their boundless enthusiasm and the need to look carefully at the other components of their life.

Being an entrepreneur means a constant balancing act. Entrepreneurs often miss out on the close relationships and family life that ladder-people can find easier to master. Families can get a raw deal from entrepreneurs, and their complaints need to be addressed.

This chapter itemises some of the downsides that the entrepreneur is likely to encounter. I cannot give you easy solutions, because there are none, and I don't want to offer meaningless clichés.

But you do need to look at these problems and ask yourself whether you have the mental, physical and financial resources to handle the downside of being your own boss.

There is no right or wrong answer. You have to work it out for yourself.

DOWNSIDE 1: ISOLATION

In the ladder-world, you were used to being part of a team.

On a bad day, you had a shoulder to cry on. On a good day, there was someone to give you a pat on the back. You had colleagues you could share things with. You were used to seeking — and receiving — validation from others before you began a task.

Now that you have your own business, you're the one who must decide when to initiate actions. It can be a lonely place. Being an entrepreneur means getting used to a more isolated existence — and it can be scary.

Another aspect of this isolation is self-doubt. Sometimes, just sometimes, even hard-core entrepreneurs entertain thoughts of taking salaried work.

It is a rare own-boss who doesn't occasionally furtively scan the recruitment pages, "just to see what's on offer". I still find myself doing it sometimes, even though the likelihood of my rejoining the ladder-world is remote.

But not too many years ago — after 20 years as a freelance entrepreneur — an offer did come my way. For about a week, I seriously contemplated the option of financial stability instead of the uncertain future I was facing at that time. I know now that such a move would have been disastrous, but to pretend that the temptation isn't there would be fooling myself.

DOWNSIDE 2: NEGATIVE FEEDBACK FROM FAMILY AND FRIENDS

Our journey from the ladder to doing our own thing rarely happens in isolation. Spouses, parents, friends and even children are part of the equation.

"You call that a real job?" is the sort of comment you may have to endure.

"How could you be so irresponsible?" is another.

You can tell that people are muttering behind your back: "When will he come to his senses?"

I once knew a singer/songwriter who went on to achieve great artistic and commercial success.

Long before he became a household name, I met his mother in the neighbourhood store. "I don't understand him", she wailed. "He sits all day long in his basement, writing songs. Why can't he get a real job?"

She probably echoed the thoughts of many a desperate ladder mother. A real job means a ladder-job. Anything else, and there's something wrong with you.

If you leave a ladder-job, but stay in the same profession (for example, you leave an accounting firm to set up on your own), the reaction of your family will be bad enough. You will be branded as a risk-taker, inconsiderate, gambling with the family silver.

If, however, you insist on following some harebrained notion of starting your own business in a field no one has ever heard of, your mental faculties will be seriously brought into question.

DOWNSIDE 3: NEGATIVE FEEDBACK FROM THE BUSINESS WORLD

You will be unpleasantly surprised to discover that not everyone is as supportive of your decision to become an entrepreneur and open your own business as you expected.

I'm afraid that this comes with the territory. Anyone who has ever attempted something original has had to withstand an element of ridicule. They probably laughed at the first steam engine too.

"A new idea is delicate. It can be killed by
a sneer or a yawn, or worried to death by
a frown on the right person's brow."

— Charles Brower

When you worked in the ladder-world, negative feedback about your employer did not devastate you. It wasn't about you personally.

Now that you're the boss of your own company, you will have to learn how to handle direct negative feedback. There will be people who doubt your business dream. Potential customers who don't appreciate your brilliance. Suppliers who don't believe you are credit-worthy. Bankers who laugh at your application for a start-up loan.

You will need all your optimism, tenacity and communication skills to counter this negativity. And it won't be easy.

DOWNSIDE 4: CASH FLOW

When you worked in the ladder-world, money was finite. There were few surprises. You knew in advance what you earned, and you knew each month that your salary would appear regularly as clockwork in your bank account.

As an entrepreneur, especially in the early days, you don't know from day to day what your cash flow is going to be.

You will make the sad discovery that not everyone likes to pay for what they buy, however satisfied they were when you delivered the goods or the services. Money that you were convinced was going to come in ("I signed and sent the cheque personally three days ago") doesn't materialise.

DOWNSIDE 5: NON-PAYMENT

Cash-flow problems can kill your business, and no amount of chutzpah or tenacity will help in really extreme circumstances.

You will have to face situations where you never see the money you are owed. Clients can disappear, either through insolvency or they simply up and run. Some clients point-blank refuse to pay, under some pretext or other.

Sometimes the only way to get your money is via litigation, which may prove more expensive than the sum owed. Some unscrupulous clients know this and exploit it. And in the meantime, you are being pressured by your suppliers and your bank to pay them what you owe. Not to mention your employees who need their salaries.

The only advice I can offer is: Be careful. If you have even the slightest doubt about a client's ability to pay, demand a down-payment. Don't let any client get account for too large a proportion of your business — we have seen too many suppliers go under when their major clients pull the plug.

DOWNSIDE 6: CHASING PAYMENT

In the ladder-world, collecting money due for services rendered or goods sold was someone else's job. You did your work, someone else chased the client for payment.

As an entrepreneur, it is now your responsibility to persuade clients to pay you for the work you did. And you will swiftly discover that some clients' payment ethic makes Scrooge look like a philanthropist.

Collecting money owed is your lifeline. You cannot afford not to give it high priority. If you think you'd be too embarrassed to chase up debts owed you, and you don't like the idea of paying a debt-collection agency to do it, just remember: this is business, not personal. From the moment you sold your product or service, this money belongs to you, not to your client. This is **your** money. It is owed to you. This is your money. It is yours by right.

DOWNSIDE 7: YOU'RE NOT FEELING WELL

When ladder-people don't feel well, they stay at home. They get doctor's notes. They get sick leave. The department and the company will survive without them.

When you become an entrepreneur, you will learn to regard "not feeling well" as something you dread. You'll be torn between wanting to work and wanting to rest. You'll find yourself battling between the urge to sleep it off and the urge to carry on regardless.

Be careful. Ignoring health problems can boomerang on you. You may be better off absenting yourself from the office for three days than to be at half-strength for three weeks.

DOWNSIDE 8: VACATIONS — WHAT ARE THEY?

In the ladder-world, you get paid vacations. And sometimes lots of them.

As an entrepreneur, you get only what you give yourself. And that is often precious little. You'll feel that there's something wrong about taking time off. You'll feel that taking a vacation from your own business is like stealing from the family piggy-bank.

You probably have less problem in okaying the expenditure of €5,000 on a new computer system for the business than spending €500 on a week's holiday.

DOWNSIDE 9: PUBLIC HOLIDAYS

Except in exceptional circumstances, you can be sure that on public holidays in the ladder-world, you won't be working.

As an entrepreneur, you'll find yourself tempted to use the quiet time of a public holiday, when the phones aren't ringing, to sort out all those things that have piled up. Your workload doesn't disappear on public holidays. And before you know it, you'll be working through Christmas Day and New Year's Day to catch up.

DOWNSIDE 10: SPENDING DECISIONS

In the ladder-world, big questions about spending priorities were taken elsewhere in the company. It was someone else's job to worry about it. Your department needed a new software package costing a couple of thousand? You put in an application, it was eventually approved, and there it was.

All of a sudden, these decisions are yours. You'll suddenly realise that there's never a good time to spend money.

But some decisions can't be put off — and you'll have to take the plunge anyway.

Chapter 11

Ten Fun Bits About Being Your Own Boss

It's always a good idea to look at some of the problems you might face before you examine the benefits.

But this chapter is about the fun bits. You will notice that some of the parameters are the same as in the previous chapter. This is no coincidence. Being your own boss can be both lonely and exhilarating. Having to make financial decisions can be both frightening and empowering.

Let's look at some of the good things about being your own boss.

1. YOU GET TO MAKE THE DECISIONS

In the ladder-world, you probably encountered plenty of situations where you could not believe how inept the decision-making was. "Are they blind?", you asked yourself about your bosses. "Can't they see where this will lead?"

Now, at last, it's your turn.

It can be a very heady experience, suddenly being able to make really fundamental decisions about everything. The premises. The staffing. The equipment. The layout. The name of the company. The logo. The letterheads. The website.

You get to put your personal stamp on absolutely everything. And it's great!

2. You're Allowed to do Nothing

There are precious few ladder-jobs where you can sit at your desk and be seen to be doing nothing. It doesn't look right and it doesn't feel right.

Now imagine that you are sitting in your own office. You are musing. Mulling something over. Or just giving your mind a little break after working on something taxing (no pun intended).

Whether you are surrounded by your own employees, or you are working alone, there's something that at last you are allowed to do: absolutely nothing!

No more having to look as if you're busy. No more having to score brownie points. No more having to impress anyone. Just sit there and muse for as long as you like. You can even spread the newspaper all over your desk. You can read the sports pages and not just the business pages. You can play a computer game. You can look at your favourite jokes website. You're in charge now, enjoy it.

3. You Can Play Hooky

Just imagine the look of puzzlement and horror that would cross your supervisor's face in a ladder-job if you announced in the middle of the afternoon that you felt like popping out to browse around a music store for a CD. It's just not done, is it?

But when you have your own business, you can work when there is work to be done, and you can take off whenever you feel like it — even if the work isn't finished.

You decide the priorities. If you want to take time off, you don't have to call in sick. You don't have to feel guilty.

"Every now and then, go away, have a little relaxation. For when you come back to your work, your judgement will be surer."

— Leonardo da Vinci

The only person you owe any explanation to is yourself — and if you're smart, you'll go easy on yourself. Feel like a stroll in the park? Just do it. A lunchtime concert? No problem. A siesta because you worked late into the night? That's your privilege. Go shopping. Go to a museum. Attend a course or lecture. It's your call.

Case Study

Eve was a young freelance website designer who worked from home. She had a very healthy workload, and was constantly having to meet impossible deadlines.

She decided to ease the pressure by attending a cookery class. Every Wednesday morning for 10 weeks, she closed her office and cycled across town to the class. She simply scheduled this into her day, and told clients in advance that she would be unavailable at that time.

The result was that Eve reduced the stress on herself, her clients learned to live with her weekly absence, and her cooking prowess improved. This was a classic win-win-win situation.

Feel like pampering yourself? Go and get a facial. Get your hair done. Go to the gym. Find another entrepreneur to play squash with in the middle of the day. And if you're a soloist, with no one waiting for you in the office, you can even decide not to go in at all today.

4. YOU CHOOSE WHOM TO WORK WITH

A major plus about being an entrepreneur is that at last you can exercise choice when it comes to whom you work with.

You will no longer have to put up with that arrogant and impertinent client. You are no longer bound to work with that unpleasant and unreliable supplier. You no longer have to accept the ineptitude of your office assistant.

From now on, you get to choose to work with people who brighten up your day, not cast a shadow over it. And if you're not comfortable with the client, the supplier, the employee — get rid of them.

Tell the client you won't be working with him in the future. Tell the supplier you are moving your custom elsewhere. Tell your employee that that's it.

Because when it comes to your own business, you can't afford to work with anyone — inside or outside your company — who isn't on your side.

5. You Choose Where You Work

To work at home or to rent an office? This is the question that many new entrepreneurs face when they first start out. The good news is that you now have much more control over how you wish to integrate your business and personal life.

Those of you that intend to rent office premises will have more say in determining how long your daily commute will be. Others might welcome the opportunity to work from home, at least to begin with.

I have tried several combinations. When I first started out as a freelance copywriter, I couldn't wait to have my own office outside the home. Somehow, an office with its own address felt more like a real business.

After a few years, when I no longer employed staff, I got to thinking that it would be neat to live and work in the same place. I was also keen to save the hour's commute each way to and from work.

Most people who decide to live and work in the same place convert part of their home into an office-space. I decided to do the reverse. I built a sleeping gallery (a sort of glorified bunk bed) above my desk, and for years I lived in my work-space instead of working in my living-space. And the arrangement worked, even though my sons (who had already left home) thought it was weird for their dad to live in a tree-house, as they called it.

Now, for the first time, I'm actually working in a dedicated office-space in my home, and I love it. (Of course, it takes a special type of partner to put up with the special type of mess this can introduce into a home.)

6. You're Free to Follow Your Imagination

Being an entrepreneur is about the freedom to use all you talents, to utilise all your faculties, to follow your own initiatives, to pursue your own ideas, to rely on your own imagination. It is also the freedom to change direction whenever you want.

"The thing you really believe in always happens . . . and the belief in a thing makes it happen."

— Frank Lloyd Wright

If you want to create a company with employer/employee relationships that are different from anything ever tried — you are free to follow your whim.

If you want to use ethical criteria in choosing staff, clients or suppliers, you can do it with impunity — and you won't be the first, either. J.C. Penney called his first retail outlets Golden Rule Stores, because he insisted that his employees never touched alcohol or tobacco.

7. You Decide When to Take a Vacation

Being your own boss means you get to choose when to take a vacation.

You are no longer bound by ladder-think, which often results in millions of people taking their vacations at the same time of year. You can stagger your vacations.

Travel off-season (when you will have less crowds and less of a hole in your pocket.)

Case Study

Melanie ran an e-commerce site that specialised in hampers. Her busiest season was in the run-up to Christmas and the New Year. She and her staff would work round the clock to fill orders, and she would always arrive at the Christmas meal in an advanced state of stress. Her children, her spouse and her parents all got a raw deal.

One year, Melanie had a brainwave. She informed everyone that she was postponing Christmas, which they would all celebrate on the 15th of January. She booked a hotel (paying low off-peak rates) for the weekend, and organised a party for family and friends. Melanie ended up enjoying a stress-free vacation, and spent more quality time with her family than ever before.

You don't need to ask permission for a day off to attend a wedding. You don't owe any explanation to anyone if you want to take two, three or even more vacations a year.

You can also exercise more imagination in choice of vacation venue. Without the peer pressure of work colleagues ("Why don't we all take our families to the Canaries together, wouldn't it be fun?"), you can now go to exotic places. Out-of-the-way places, or places near home that you never visited.

8. You Dictate Your Own Schedule

As an entrepreneur, you decide how to fill your schedule. Being your own boss allows you to devote time and thought to non-business activities.

You decide how many hours you're going to spend on what. You decide how much time to devote to your family, to your interests, to your extra-curricular activities.

At a certain point after setting up my own first business, I joined my local drama group, and discovered a long-dormant acting talent. Although I enjoyed the acting, I was more interested in the promotional and organisational side of things.

I took over responsibility for the drama group's publicity. I opened a dialogue with other "rival" drama groups. I organised a national festival, which turned into an annual event. I wrote and edited a national newsletter. I founded a national association of drama groups, and even joined the executive board of the International Amateur Theatre Association.

The point about all this activity, which I conducted from my desk, is that no one could tell me to stop doing theatre work and get on with my paid work.

Yes, I might be wealthier today if I'd spent less time on theatre business, but this was my choice, and I loved every moment of it. I decided how much time to devote to a cause I believed in. I made my own decisions on how to divide my work- and non-work-related activities.

If I'd been accountable to a ladder boss, I never would have had the freedom or resources to make this decision.

9. YOU EXPERIENCE A DEEP SENSE OF PRIDE

There is nothing quite like the sense of ownership and pride you experience when you have your own business. It is wonderful to be engaged in something that you can be truly proud of, knowing that it's yours, that you created it, that you're responsible for its success.

You will find that owning your business defines you. You will experience the special thrill of providing a service or manufacturing a product that people want. You will look at your achievements and feel an almost parental pride.

The following story illustrates this nicely.

The Mountain

There were two warring tribes in the Andes. One tribe lived in the lowlands and the other high in the mountains.

One day, the mountain people invaded the lowlanders. They kidnapped a lowlander baby and took the infant with them back up into the mountains.

The lowlanders didn't know how to climb the mountain. They didn't know any of the trails that the mountain people used. They didn't know where to find the mountain people or how to track them in the steep terrain.

Nevertheless, the lowlanders sent out a party of their strongest men to climb the mountain and bring the baby home.

The men tried first one method of climbing and then another. They tried one trail and then another. But after several days of effort, they had only climbed a few hundred feet.

Feeling hopeless and helpless, the lowlander men decided that they weren't going to make it, and prepared to return to their village below.

As they were packing their gear for the descent, they saw a figure emerge from the mist. As the figure came towards them, they saw that it was the baby's mother. She was coming down the mountain — and here they were, unable to climb any further.

The lowlanders then noticed that she had the baby strapped to her back. They greeted her and said:

"We couldn't climb this mountain. How did you do it, when we, the strongest and most able men in the village, couldn't?"

She shrugged her shoulders and said:

"It wasn't your baby."

10. You Can't Be Fired!

Need I say more!

Chapter 12

Hats Off to Entrepreneurs

One of the first things you realise as an entrepreneur is that you must learn to juggle with lots of different functions when you're your own boss. At least to start with, entrepreneurs have to do it all. You have to be prepared to do any job, however menial. If you become a soloist or run a small business, you will have to juggle even more hats for even longer.

In order to illustrate this point in my entrepreneur workshops, I bring in a collection of hats, berets, caps — anything I can lay my hands on. Each hat represents a "hat" that entrepreneurs have to wear during the course of their work. I then proceed to try and wear as many as I can, one piled on top the other.

It always comes as a surprise to realise just how many different hats they will have to wear when they open their new business:

- CEO/Managing Director
- PA to the CEO
- Telephonist
- Receptionist

- Sales Manager
- Marketing Director
- Advertising Manager
- Financial Director
- Office Manager
- Personnel Manager
- Customer Support Manager
- Recruitment Officer
- Payroll Clerk
- Company Spokesman
- Head of PR
- IT Manager
- Production Manager
- Warehouse Manager
- Complaints Manager
- Safety Manager
- R&D Manager
- Chief Buyer
- Strategist
- Business Manager
- New Business Manager
- Training Manager
- Property Manager
- Janitor
- Handyman
- Canteen Manager
- Maintenance Manager.

My purpose is not to scare you. But it's something you ought to be aware of. At any given time, you will be wearing one or more hat. In the space of a few seconds, you will switch hat several times. Imagine the following scenario.

A prospective client comes to visit your one-person office. You welcome him, offer him coffee, and sit down to chat. He asks you questions about your service or product, prices, delivery times, and so on. While you are talking, you answer a call from someone answering your ad for a position in your new company. As you put the phone down, the bulb goes and the room is plunged into darkness. While you're fixing the bulb, your new business cards are delivered.

In that five-minute sequence, how many hats did you wear? Let's re-run the scenario:

A prospective client comes to visit your one-man office. You welcome him (RECEPTIONIST), offer him coffee (CANTEEN MANAGER), and sit down to chat (CEO). You answer questions about your service or product (SALES PERSON, MARKETING MANAGER), prices (FINANCIAL DIRECTOR), delivery times (PRODUCTION MANAGER), and so on (CUSTOMER CARE MANAGER). While you are talking, you answer a call (TELEPHONIST) from someone answering your ad (ADVERTISING MANAGER) for a position in your new company (RECRUITMENT OFFICER). As you put the phone down, the bulb goes and the room is plunged into darkness, and you apologise to your guest (COMPANY SPOKESMAN). While you're fixing the bulb (JANITOR), your new business cards (PR MANAGER) are delivered (WAREHOUSE MANAGER).

So many hats — and all in just five minutes.

The good news is that you become adept at juggling, and feel a sense of pride in being able to master this particular skill.

Chapter 13

Hop On, Hop Off

This chapter is about hopping off the ladder and hopping back on again.

However strong your gut feeling that you want to get off the ladder and start your own business, the real world can sometimes be very cruel.

You may hit a run of bad luck. Things can go pear-shaped, and a combination of bouncing cheques, delayed payments from clients, a turndown in orders, or slow market penetration of a new product or service, can precipitate a cash-flow crisis that forces you to close the business.

Businesses can fail for a variety of reasons:

You may have chosen the worst possible time to get off the ladder.

Seamus was a cabbie in Dublin. He left his job as a driver with a large freight company to buy his own taxi. He paid €80,000 for the plates — just months before government deregulation reduced the value of the plates to a few hundred euros. He was left with huge debts.

**You may have chosen to go into a business sector
that was undergoing rapid change.**

*Lisa left her ladder job to buy a stationery supply
shop. She took out loans, she brought in members of
the family, and she bought lots of stock. Two months
later, a nationwide chain of stationery superstores
opened a new store 50 yards down the road. Her
turnover was decimated, and she had to close the
business with heavy losses.*

**You may have discovered that the reality did not
match up to your dreams.**

*Stuart bought the mini-market that he had previously
managed. Soon after taking over the business, he was
hit by a spate of pilfering by the staff. He discovered
that he had been more comfortable running the store
on behalf of the owner, than owning the store himself.*

*He sold the business at a loss, and found a job as
spokesman and fundraiser for an international
organisation. He has almost total autonomy in his new
job, and he's as happy as can be.*

You may have become too reliant on a single client.

> *Eleanor left the large graphic design studio where she was employed in order to start her own design business. She had been emboldened to move off the ladder because she had secured a really big client. The workload was huge, and she took on a team of designers.*
>
> *But, less than a year after opening her studio, her big client went into liquidation - and Eleanor was left with debts that forced her own business to fold.*

You may not be a good businessperson.

> *Even if you have entrepreneurial blood streaming through your veins, you may not have a head for business. Thomas is a gifted chef. Encouraged by his success in supplying catered meals to friends, he decided to leave his job on a newspaper to start his own catering business.*
>
> *But he simply had no idea how to price his services. He was charging less for his meals than they cost him to make. Within a short time he had lost thousands, and the business folded.*

Whatever the reason for a business failure, it's OK to cut your losses and hop back on the ladder. There is no shame in taking refuge in the ladder-world while you lick your wounds.

Some of you will be scared by the experience of your own business failure, and vow never to try such foolishness again. More of you are likely to keep an eye out for the next opportunity to hop off the ladder again to be your own boss.

And some of you might end up hopping off and hopping back onto the ladder-world quite a few times in your life. And that's OK too.

The emergence of intrapreneurs (see box) makes this hopping on and off even easier. It is likely that we will see more and more intrapreneurs hopping off the ladder to become entrepreneurs, and more and more entrepreneurs hopping back on the ladder to become intrapreneurs.

Intrapreneurs

The ladder-world has discovered that the knee-jerk adherence of ladder managers at every level (including the very top) to the idea that everything the company does is right, can stultify creativity and independent thought.

To combat this, many ladders have embraced and nurtured the intrapreneur concept — someone who possesses the qualities of an entrepreneur, but expresses them while remaining an employee within an employment structure.

The encouragement of intrapreneurism is a sign that the ladder world wishes to emulate the entrepreneurial spirit.

> *Ladders are worried that, in today's job market, if they don't give ambitious players more autonomy, these bright people will leave the ladder-world and go into business on their own. The nurturing of intrapreneurs is highly functional for the ladder-world.*
>
> *Intrapreneurism can also solve the dilemma for people with an independent streak who cannot bring themselves to take the plunge and start their own business.*

Remember, it's your decision. It's your life. You can hop off and on as often as you want — until you find what you want. Don't let anyone usurp your role in deciding what you should do.

Chapter 14

Ten DON'Ts

We've looked at the fun bits of being your own boss, and we've looked at some of the problems you could meet. This chapter assumes that you're still aboard the entrepreneurial train, and offers you some friendly advice about things to watch out for.

These don'ts are easier said than done, but they are worth bearing in mind as you commence your entrepreneurial journey.

1. DON'T UNDERESTIMATE THE LONELINESS OF THE LONG-DISTANCE ENTREPRENEUR

Running your own business is a lonely occupation. The buck stops with you. If you are thinking of going it alone, ask yourself whether you can take it emotionally.

It can be tough being on your own, and families are often more of a hindrance than a help in reducing your sense of isolation. They get fed up with always hearing about your business problems — and anyway they only hear half of the problems, because most of the time you're trying to shield them from what is really on your mind.

"Top of mountain great place, but very lonely."

— Confucius

No matter how big or how small your operation, the sense of isolation is among your most formidable psychological as well as professional challenges. You will discover that one of the best sources of support for an entrepreneur is another entrepreneur.

The only people who really understand what it's like at the coal-face of entrepreneurial effort are fellow entrepreneurs.

When you want to moan, complain and bitch about clients, suppliers, the taxman, the bank — or about the fact that your family isn't giving you the moral support you need — you'll find that only another entrepreneur will really understand. Only another entrepreneur can console you when business is lousy, and can tell you yes, it's normal to worry about your business.

I am lucky to have one such entrepreneur friend. We regularly swap notes on the ups and downs of our respective businesses.

Happily, we both have supportive partners, but as much as we love them dearly, they are still ladder-people. They cheer us on when we're ahead, and they commiserate with us when we're down. But they don't really want to hear a blow-by-blow account of what the marketing manager of our biggest client said to us as he informed us that he was taking the work in-house.

Case Study

Julie is an artist who had been in business on her own for a couple of years.

In one of my entrepreneurial workshops, she told us that every few months, she feels the need to phone her entrepreneurial friend Annette who lives and works abroad.

"I call her just to hear her tell me how great I am," Julie told us. "No matter how well I am doing, it's great every once in a while to get a praise fix from someone who really understands."

Another way of combating isolation is to join an entrepreneur network. When you meet other entrepreneurs on a regular basis, formally or informally, you'll discover new opportunities for understanding and support.

2. Don't Let Experts or Banks Kill off Your Special Idea

Don't let anyone create doubt in your mind. Banks and so-called experts are masters at sowing seeds of doubt in your mind. Don't let them?"

"Are you sure there's a market for this?" "Has anyone else succeeded in this kind of venture?" "Have you thought this through properly?" they ask.

But it's not just banks.

The Wright Brothers' own father told his sons to stop wasting their time trying to fly. Even Thomas Edison tried to dissuade his friend Henry Ford from getting into the mass production of motor cars.

Remember: the people who discourage your new ideas before you've had a chance to nurture and develop them are usually ladder-people. That's why they are sitting on their side of the desk in their ladder-job, and why you're sitting on your side of the desk, raring to get on with your dream. It's their job to prick your entrepreneurial balloon.

Case Study

A year before I moved to Ireland, I had dinner with a top Dublin banker to whom I'd been introduced. The object of the exercise was to discuss my chances of success in setting up a freelance copywriting business in Ireland, along the same lines as my Israeli venture.

I was not asking him for a loan, and in any case he was not in commercial banking. All I wanted was advice and pointers in the right direction from a representative of the business world. I explained my marketing strategy, and described who I thought my clients would be.

The best that he could muster was to tell me that "they had already invented the wheel in Ireland". The sub-text was clear. "You've nothing new to offer. Copywriters are in plentiful supply here. You'll never get your business off the ground."

> Luckily, I also met with professionals in my own field, including other freelance copywriters. They encouraged me. They saw the potential. The banker's ignorance of the scene had been no barrier to his willingness to spout negativity.
>
> (I didn't know whether to laugh or to cry when I later read that this same banker was hauled in by the police for questionable business practices.)

"There are always people who haven't done anything who spend their lives warning others not to do anything."

— Bernie Ecclestone

In the face of negative thinking, the trick is to stay focused, to remain dedicated to your idea, to remain passionate about your business. Keep telling yourself that your instincts are healthy, that whatever you based your decision on is sound, no matter what anyone else says.

Just go for it. Don't let anyone divert you from your vision, don't get too stuck on details, and protect your creative thoughts from the naysayers who tell you it won't work.

3. Don't Overdo the Adrenaline Bit!

Many entrepreneurs pride themselves on their ability to thrive in crisis situations. They love the thrill of surmounting challenges. When faced with deadlines and disasters, their pulse races, their adrenaline zooms around their system, and they rush into the fray. They love having to juggle lots of tasks at the same time.

All this is fine, but . . . don't overdo it. Don't burn yourself out. Being able to respond vigorously to problems is a healthy attribute. Being manic at all times is less desirable. Your judgements will be impaired if everything is a rush, if everything is an emergency, if everything is a crisis.

4. Don't Assume that Being Your *OWN* Boss Necessarily Makes You a *GOOD* Boss

One of the problems about being your own boss is that you are expected to automatically know how to be someone else's boss. But in truth, many of you who start your own businesses have never had a "good boss" as a role model. On the contrary, your decision to start your own company is often motivated by the fact you could never get on with your boss, supervisor or manager. So how are you meant to know how a good boss behaves?

I offer no simple solution to this dilemma. Some of you will have to add basic management skills to your shopping list of what you need to learn, and I hope you turn out to be exemplary bosses yourselves.

You might conclude that however keen you are to run your own show, you might not be particularly good at being someone else's boss.

Case Study

When Jeremy first opened his own management consultancy outfit, he had fantasies of running an international organisation. He envisaged offices in several world capitals, and chose London as his launching pad.

In the course of building up his London office, Jeremy realised that he would have to trim his dreams. The main reason was that he discovered that he was not very good at dealing with staff.

He would get impatient. He would get embarrassed if he failed to explain adequately what he wanted done — and then get frustrated when the results were not what he expected. He had a problem with the receptionist reading a newspaper, even if at that moment there was nothing else for her to do.

In short, he was not a good boss. He was not comfortable in the role of boss.

So now he works alone. He has become very streamlined, and he has mastered the art of outsourcing.

There are several labels attached to entrepreneurs who work alone with no staff. They are called freelancers. Solo operators. Sole traders. Soloists. Sole proprietors. Consultants. Contractors. Lone wolfs.

They are a sort of hybrid breed, business owners whose enterprises support a single salary: their own.

Management guru Peter Drucker claims that taking a job in the ladder-world is risky, because the routine and limits can destroy people's creativity. He says that it is much more fun being a soloist.

Soloists are not always going to pioneer new technologies, nor do they always dream of creating the industries of tomorrow. They don't build empires, and they don't always get rich. They're more into building careers than equity. But they are driven by the same sense of excitement, enthusiasm, energy and motivation as entrepreneurs who go on to create multi-million businesses.

5. DON'T PAY ATTENTION TO EVERY TOM, DICK AND HARRIET'S OPINION

As soon as you announce your decision to start your own business, you will discover that suddenly everyone has an opinion.

Family members who themselves have failed in business are reborn as business experts. Friends who have never ever wanted to work on their own suddenly know all the perils of entrepreneurship.

When you are planning to be your own boss, you will find it's sad truth: some of the worst advice can emanate from those closest to you, especially those you live with. When you seek advice on your entrepreneurial business from ladder friends and family, remember that they are ladder-centric. Their advice will come from their ladder experience.

> *"Beware of people who play the devil's advocate — they want to show you why something won't succeed."*
>
> — Wally Amos

You have to remember that many entrepreneurial adventures are based on new ideas. Advice based on the conventional ladder way of doing things is doomed to clash with these new ideas.

Remember too that people close to you have their own agendas when they give you advice. Make allowances for the fact that the ladder-world is more used to saying "But ..." than "Wow!". Learn to walk the fine line between sticking to your guns and gently but firmly rejecting unsolicited or tainted advice.

A useful strategy in situations where either option is acceptable is to ask only for advice on specifics: "Darling, do you think I should dress casual or elegant at the presentation?" is a safer bet than asking an open-ended question like "Do you think I'm doing the right thing?".

6. DON'T UNDERMINE YOUR OWN WORTH

Being an entrepreneur means recognising your own talents. Acknowledging your own worth. Don't ever give in to the belief that you have less to offer than even the top person in your field. Whatever line of business you intend to go into — just go for it.

Acknowledging your own worth also extends into the realm of salary. Every Teach Yourself book and every entrepreneurial programme will tell you that you need to keep your personal earnings down while the business builds itself.

Yes, but . . .

As any accountant will tell you, budding entrepreneurs seldom pay themselves as much as they should. Which is strange, really. After all, if you want to attract top people to your business, you know that you'll have to offer top salaries.

But you yourself are one of the top people! So why not pay yourself accordingly?

The story below is not really about entrepreneurship, but it teaches a nice lesson about knowing your own worth.

The Governor and the Gas Station Attendant

The Governor of Texas, then Mark White, was taking a relaxing drive through the open Texas countryside with his wife. They found themselves in the area where Mrs. White grew up.

As they pulled into a gas station, the Governor noticed that his wife was a little nervous. He didn't say anything, but when the gas station attendant came out to their car, the Governor could not help noticing that his wife and the attendant seemed surprised to see each other. They acted with that awkwardness people have when they've been intimate in the past.

Governor White pretended not to notice. They left the gas station and continued back down the highway. For a long time, they remained silent. Mrs. White kept looking out the window, staring out into the distance. The Governor was considerate and patient, and continued to drive in silence. After almost an hour, he said:

"Honey, I couldn't help noticing how you and that gas station attendant looked at each other. You used to be involved with him, didn't you?"

"Well, yes," she responded, quietly.

"Well, I guess I know how you feel", said the Governor. "You probably needed some space, right?"

"Yes," she said again.

"And I guess you were probably thinking", continued the Governor, "how different your two lives had become. You were probably thinking that if you had married him, then you'd be the wife of a gas station attendant now, instead of the wife of the Governor. Right?"

"Well, no", answered Mrs. White. "Actually I was thinking that he'd be the Governor now."

7. DON'T BELIEVE THAT YOU'RE EVER TOO OLD OR TOO YOUNG TO BECOME AN ENTREPRENEUR

People often ask: When is the right time to start your own business?

Well, there is no "perfect" time in life to start on the road to business ownership. There are successful entrepreneurs from age 10 to age 80. Age is no obstacle when someone is determined to succeed and has faith in their abilities.

Case Study

Michael's folks wanted him to be a doctor, but he had other ideas. By the age of 12, he had established his own mail order business selling stamps, and was soon making thousands of dollars. While still in high school, he made $18,000 selling newspaper subscriptions. His selling urge did not desert him when he went to college, where he sold $180,000 in his first month.

Michael is Michael Dell, of Dell Computer Corporation.

From childhood, he knew that he wanted to run his own business, one that would be as big as IBM. Now IBM competes with Dell.

Case Study

Doris Drucker is the wife of the management guru Peter Drucker.

Doris was in her 80s when she got it into her head to start her first-ever business, guided by the Biblical motto: "If not now, when?"

She came up with a completely new product that no one had thought of, did the research, had a prototype built, worked her hide off, sold hundreds of products, had lots of fun — and even made a tidy profit.

---

8. DON'T EVER APOLOGISE FOR SUCCEEDING OR FOR HAVING FUN

It is so easy to succumb to other people's negativity. Lots of killjoys out there would have you believe that work and fun are incompatible. Lots of people are uncomfortable with the enthusiasm of entrepreneurs. These people belong to what I term the "Why bother, nothing makes one happy anyway" brigade.

Someone emailed me these really useful tips on How to be Unhappy.

How to Be Unhappy

— *Don't just **let** little things bother you, **make** them bother you.*

— *Lose your perspective on things and keep it lost: don't put first things first.*

— *Find yourself a good worry, one about which you can do nothing.*

— *Constantly condemn yourself and others for not achieving perfection.*

— *Be right. Be always right. Be the only one who is always right. Be rigid in your rightness.*

— *Don't trust or believe people, or accept them as anything but their worst and weakest.*

— *Be suspicious, and insist that everyone else always has hidden motives.*

— *Always compare yourself unfavourably to others. This guarantees instant misery.*

— *Make sure that you take personally everything that happens to you.*

— *Don't give yourself whole-heartedly to anyone or anything.*

You never have to apologise for starting your own business, for making a success of it, or for being one smart cookie.

And don't ever apologise for having fun at work. Your enthusiasm is the ace up your sleeve, your optimism is the battery that drives you to levels of energy that can leave others gasping for breath.

> *"Knowledge is power —*
> *enthusiasm pulls the switch."*
>
> — Steve Droke

I met an assertiveness trainer who claimed that the single most important thing she teaches is that it's OK to say "No" without having to explain.

You don't have to explain your decision to start your own business. You can if you want, but you don't have to. And you certainly don't need to apologise.

9. DON'T FORGET TO HAVE A LIFE

John Teeling is always willing to share his entrepreneurial experiences with other entrepreneurs.

John's latest message is "Don't forget to have a life." He says that there's a danger that entrepreneurs who invest all their emotional and physical resources in their business can wake up after 20 years to discover that they have missed all the fun.

Sometimes, says Teeling, it's just a good idea to pull back the adrenaline lever. Create a balance between the demands of work and having fun.

Take the day off. Do something totally non-work-related. When you come back, the crises won't have disappeared, but your ability to handle things will have improved.

Many years ago, I remember talking to a client of mine, the boss of an advertising agency. He told me that every single evening, he watched movies on a giant screen at home. I was shocked. Why would someone openly admit to such a "waste of time"?

It wasn't until I was a little older and a little wiser that I realised that he was the smart one. By creating a non-work-related outlet, he was getting the best of both worlds.

*I never did a day's work in my life —
it was all fun.*

— Thomas Alva Edison

10. DON'T SLAM THE DOOR ON THE LADDER WORLD

Never burn your bridges. When you quit your ladder-job, don't slam the door. Be smart. Leave with dignity. Exercise a bit of strategic and tactical thinking, and leave the door open for longer-term dialogue.

Just because you're leaving does not mean the relationship has to end. You never know when your paths will cross again. You might need the ladder and the ladder might need you. You could be called in as a consultant. You might be able to use their contacts.

That's why it's not a good idea to make phone calls on company time or send CVs through the company's email — without squaring this first with your boss.

You may also want to consider a re-entry strategy. You have nothing to lose by discussing a "What if . . . ?" scenario with your boss.

Case Study

Patrick was a young computer programmer who was fired from his ladder-job when the department was downsized. Luckily, he quickly found a new job similar to the previous job, but on a higher salary.

Three months into his new job, his old boss called him up. "Can you help me out with a few projects?" Patrick agreed to work on a consultancy basis.

He was totally familiar with the material, and he found that he could work on the projects in the evenings. He also discovered that he could command much higher rates for the consultancy work than he received as an employee. Emboldened by the volume of consultancy work, he started pitching for more freelance work. His workload became so great that he left his ladder-job and worked full-time as a consultant.

If Patrick had not left his previous ladder-job on good terms, and if he had not left the door open to future developments, he might never have taken the plunge to set up on his own.

Chapter 15

Get Out There and Sock It to Them

We started this book on a quest to explore the non-skill aspects of being an entrepreneur.

We defined an entrepreneur as anyone who feels the urge to be their own boss and who starts their own business.

We defined the ladder-world as the world of employment where a regular salary defines workplace relationships.

We asked whether nature or nurture produces entrepreneurs, and we looked at why so many ladder-people come to regard the ladder-world as a health hazard.

We examined the triggers that can push you off the ladder, and we discussed the process of choosing in which business to make your mark.

We itemised the prerequisites for starting your own business, and we drew comparisons between the ladder and the non-ladder-worlds.

We took a sober look at some of the bad things that can happen when you are your own boss, and then we looked at the fun bits of going it alone.

We congratulated the entrepreneur's ability to wear so many hats, and we looked at why people sometimes hop on and off the ladder.

Finally, we looked at some useful tips about potential obstacles in your way to becoming your own boss.

If you have successfully navigated the mental transition from ladder-think to entrepreneur-think, the hard part is already behind you.

By now you'll have a better appreciation of what being your own boss is about. You'll know more about the pain and more about the gain.

Now comes the easy part — learning the skills. So get out there and sock it to them. With fire in your belly, you'll be able to sail through the skills thing.

Read books like Gary Joseph Grappo's high-octane *Start Your Own Business in 30 Days*.

Be inspired by the stories of other entrepreneurs, like the *Sunday Times* My First Break series.

Go on courses. Seek professional advice — because the best killer idea will only succeed if you remember to get the business side of the equation right.

In your dealings with bankers and other ladder-people, never forget that you embrace a different belief system from them. Mollify them a little by learning their vocabulary. Leave your sneakers at home and wear shoes for your meeting.

But whatever you do, don't let anyone try and change your idea or pour cold water on your plans.

Stick to your guns, and go for it.

Good luck!

Yanky's Entrepreneurial Seminars

Whether he is addressing a small seminar or a conference audience of hundreds, Yanky (usually accompanied by his ubiquitous ladder) adopts a distinctive and entertaining motivational style that brings his subject alive. Yanky's seminars include:

DO I HAVE WHAT IT TAKES TO BE MY OWN BOSS?

Targeted at people who are thinking of starting their own business, this workshop gives valuable insight into the entrepreneurial experience, helping participants understand the emotional transition from the world of employment to the world of self-employment.

IS LOSING YOUR JOB A GOOD REASON FOR STARTING YOUR OWN BUSINESS?

Redundancy can often be seen as the opportunity to go and start a business. This workshop helps people who have already lost their job or could lose their job to explore self-employment as an option, and to discover whether anger is a sufficient trigger for starting a business.

EXPLODING THE MYTH OF ON-TAP EMOTIONAL SUPPORT

It is a myth that people shouldn't even consider starting a business unless their family wholeheartedly supports the decision.

This workshop explores why the very people from whom budding entrepreneurs crave support are unable to give it, and offers tips on how spouses and partners can better understand where their entrepreneurial partners are coming from. This workshop sparked Yanky's latest book, **"My Family Doesn't Understand Me!" Coping Strategies for Entrepreneurs**.

WHATEVER POSSESSED ME TO BE MY OWN BOSS?

Many people running their own businesses feel jaded, overworked and under-appreciated. Above all, they feel lonely. They forget why they wanted to be their own boss in the first place. This workshop helps to re-motivate, re-energise and inspire owner managers of small and medium businesses.

ALL YOU NEED IS CHUTZPAH

Targeted at people who are starting their own business and at those who are part of a larger organisation, this workshop explores how to use chutzpah - a combination of nerve, bottle, cheek, gall and balls - to forge ahead of the pack.

Praise for Fire in the Belly

Your book is so motivational, and answered so many things I have been wondering about myself for years. I will also highly recommend the book to others, and I certainly hope they enjoy it as much as I did.

Nuala Acton, Director, Eventime, Ireland

You don't often find a book that walks you through things like the pros and cons of entrepreneurship. I really enjoyed it, the tone is light and easy to read. If you are seriously considering becoming your own boss, the book does a very good job in making you think about the decision to go it alone - before you jump in up to your neck.

Deiric McCann, *Cara*, Aer Lingus magazine

When I first picked up your book, I realised that every page was talking directly to me. I found myself nodding in agreement on every page. Your book emboldened me to find the courage to start my own business. I keep it with me at all times, dipping into its chapters for advice, encouragement and inspiration.

Ciara Mullen, Founder of e-nails Nail Bar

New from Yanky Fachler

"My Family Doesn't Understand Me!"

Coping Strategies for Entrepreneurs

ISBN: 1-86076-268-9

Price: €20 Format: Paperback

"Unless you have the support of your family, you are better off forgetting and foregoing any notion of starting your own business."

This message is repeated in countless books, articles, web-sites and training courses. Would-be entrepreneurs are told that, if they cannot count on family for emotional support, their entrepreneurial venture is bound to fail.

"My Family Doesn't Understand Me!" challenges the myth of on-tap family support, and offers a suite of coping strategies for the real world of Start Your Own Business.

Available in all good bookshops or direct from Oak Tree Press at **www.oaktreepress.com**.

OAK TREE PRESS

Ireland's leading business book publisher,
Oak Tree Press is increasingly an international
developer and publisher of enterprise training and
support solutions.

Oak Tree Press has developed "platforms" of Pre-
start-up, Start-up, Growth and Support content,
which include publications, websites, software,
assessment models, training, consultancy and
certification.

Oak Tree Press' enterprise training and support
solutions are in use in Ireland, the UK, USA,
Scandinavia and Eastern Europe and are available
for customisation to local situations and needs.

For further information, contact:
Ron Immink or Brian O'Kane
OAK TREE PRESS
19 Rutland Street, Cork, Ireland
T: + 353 21 431 3855   F: + 353 21 431 3496
E: info@oaktreepress.com
W: www.oaktreepress.com

www.oaktreepress.com